Railway History Series
Volume One

TWO CENTURIES OF RAILWAYS

Alan Earnshaw

Nostalgia Road Publications

CONTENTS

INTRODUCTION	3
ANCIENT APPLICATION OF RAIL	6
THE ORIGINS OF RAIL	8
THE CANAL ERA & BEYOND	13
THE STEAM RAILWAY ARRIVES	18
MOVING ON FROM THE MANIA	27
INTO THE 20TH CENTURY	33
THE RAILWAY GROUPING OF 1923	40
THE FORMATION OF BRITISH RAILWAYS	44
DOCTOR BEECHING'S AXE	49
THE YEARS OF NEGLECT	56
PRIVATISATION - A NEW FUTURE?	63

The **Nostalgia Road** Series™

is produced under licence by

Nostalgia Road Publications Ltd.
Units 5 - 8, Chancel Place, Shap Road Industrial Estate,
Kendal, Cumbria, LA9 6NZ
Tel. +44 (0)1539 738832 - Fax: +44 (0)1539 730075

designed and published by
Trans-Pennine Publishing Ltd.
PO Box 10, Appleby-in-Westmorland, Cumbria, CA16 6FA
Tel. +44 (0)17683 51053 Fax. +44 (0)17683 53558
e-mail: admin@transpenninepublishing.co.uk

and printed by
Kent Valley Colour Printers Ltd.
Kendal, Cumbria +44 (0)1539 741344

© Text: Trans-Pennine Publishing Ltd. 2005
© Photographs: Author's collection or as credited

Front Cover: *The early days of the steam locomotive are re-created at Blists Hill Victorian Town, Ironbridge where a replica of Trevithick's Coalbrookdale locomotive is pictured across the upper canal in June 2005.*

Rear Cover Top: *British Railways Standard Class steam returns to Whitby Town Station in May 2005 behind 4MT 76079, as it works the Glaisdale Express service along the Esk Valley line.*

Rear Cover Bottom: *The modern face of Britain's railways as Royal Train locomotive 67006 arrives at Appleby-in-Westmorland Station in April 2005 with Prince Charles on board.*

Title Page: *The epitome of main line British steam, captured at Birmingham New Street on 29th June 1957, as ex-LMS Black 5 departs with the 8.05am train to Newcastle.* **Michael Mensing**

This Page: *By contrast, the humble branch line train from Ballachulish is found behind ex-Caledonian design 0-4-4T 55263, at Appin on 6th July 1956.* **M. Patterson**

ALL RIGHTS RESERVED
No Part of this publication may be reproduced, stored in a retrieval system, or transmitted, in any form or by any means, electronic, mechanical, photocopying, recording or otherwise, without prior permission in writing from the publishers.
ISBN 1 903016 64 9
British Cataloguing in Publication Data
A catalogue record for this book is available from the British Library

INTRODUCTION

Railways have absorbed man's interest for at least 200 years, and thus created a phenomenon that is hard to explain. Quite why this is so is equally difficult to rationalise upon, especially in the early days of the 21st century when railways are no longer the fastest or most convenient way to travel. Yet fascinate and enthuse they certainly do, with their audience coming from across a wide spectrum of ages.

Predominantly once a male interest only, railway enthusiasm has now bridged the gender gap and quite literally appeals to every sector of society in the developed world. For some the enthusiasm centres on the excellence of mechanical or civil engineering, for others it is their commercial attraction.

Above: *The romance with the steam railway was due to the fact that, until the 1960s, it touched nearly every community, offering the chance of travel to distant horizons. Sadly, lines like that from Halwill Junction to Torrington were hardly profitable, as this view of 41312 and a one-coach train in 1962 suggests.* R. C. Riley

Others simply like trains because they take them to exciting places, a big city, a holiday, the start of a grand adventure, or back home to see loved family members. Have you ever noticed how many people, even those who profess no interest in railways, will stand by the trackside and wave at the trains passing by? Is this some kind of idiosyncrasy or a subconscious desire of the person at the trackside to exchange places with the passengers speeding by?

Trains were viewed as exciting, especially the long-distance express services, as they took people to places far removed from their every day life! They were like the magic carpets of Arabian legend, offering the ability to transport people wherever their hearts desired – even if for the majority that was simply a holiday in Blackpool or a day trip to Brighton.

Today cheap air travel conveys far more people to their holiday destinations than the railways, whilst private cars are usually the favoured alternative for weekend jaunts, but the train still has its unique form of appeal. The railway network has shrunk to a fraction of its original size, thousands of stations have been closed, and the connecting bus services introduced to replace those lost trains have long since been withdrawn and forgotten. For forty years frankly atrocious railway services have been operated upon those lines that remained open, with dirty, unpunctual trains running at times more suited to the management than the people who wanted to use them.

Even so, the love for the railways has not abated, and the enthusiasm has even grown in some areas. People, who were dismayed with the decline of the railways, the withdrawal of steam locomotives and the closing of their local line, have all done their 'bit' to help keep the world of railways alive. Locomotives and rolling stock have been saved from the scrap-heap and lovingly restored, old branch lines have been purchased and re-opened, and a massive heritage railway movement has grown up in the same four decades. Today these 'heritage' lines are big business, filling a vital role in the local tourism economy all over Britain, and can no longer be looked upon as places where enthusiasts play with trains.

Not everyone can own a real locomotive or a railway station, but tens of thousands have sought to recreate the world of railways in miniature. From tiny scales, such as Z Gauge and N Gauge, up to $7^{1}/_{2}$-inch gauge live steam, enthusiasts have rebuilt their favourite locomotives, carriages, freight vehicles and railway settings. The model railway industry is now a huge business, despite the fact that many of the suppliers are basically 'one-man-bands' or cottage industries supplying goods to the niche markets that they have identified in this area of commerce. A glance through the pages of the model railway press will show just how many small businesses are supplying this market with goods or services, and from this you can gauge just how widespread the interest in this hobby is. These people are no longer just playing with toy trains and an oval of track on the dining room table, rather they are recreating social and engineering history in a three-dimensional display form and have a great deal of fun in doing so.

The same can be said of those hardy souls standing at the end of railway platforms in all weathers, with their notebooks, pens and cameras in hand. Train-spotters are to many an objective of derision, even sympathy, yet to others they are a group of people making a dedicated and comprehensive record of the way our railways operate. Today some people call them 'anoraks', but tomorrow they might look back on them as 'social historians'; isn't it funny how time can alter our perspective on things? As a historian I often wish that train-spotters and railway photographers had been around in large numbers two centuries ago, as their records would have undoubtedly assisted my presentation of this over-view of two centuries of railway history.

In the analysis of railway history that follows, I wanted to set out some of the key stages in railway development and show how we moved from humble beginnings in the early days of the Industrial Revolution to where we stood at the end of the 20th century. This is quite a task in what is a relatively small book, but it is a topic that several people feel is much needed; especially given the fact that so many people know so little about the genesis of the transport system that they love so much. This is quite ironic really, especially when you consider that the subject of railways and the trains that run upon them is a topic upon which millions of words have been written.

For my own part I have written dozens of books (plus hundreds of articles on railway subjects), and have a library sagging under the combined weight of several hundred more. I have spent thousands of hours in archives, record offices, libraries and dingy, dusty basements collecting data, but still never found a concise overview of how the railways of Britain came to be. However, two books certainly stand out, and I can certainly recommend *The Railways of Britain* by Professor Jack Simmons, and the 1934 book *The Railway King,* by Richard S. Lambert. Another useful tool is *The Oxford Companion To British Railway History*. Yet all these tomes are weighty publications, and not ideal reading for the beginner or the person with just a casual interest.

Having for a long number of years, been involved with a series of books that provided a high quality read at a modest cover price, first with Atlantic Transport Publishers and latterly with Trans-Pennine Publishing, I wondered how we could cover this subject in a single, reasonably-priced paperback edition. The result follows, as we take you on a whistle stop tour of railway history. In places this 'express journey' is punctuated by a halt at a 'rural station' and a meander up some railway 'by-way', as I try and illustrate some general point with a specific example.

Where I have done so, I have picked on a small number of lines that make specific examples that can be linked together as they make a universal point. That is not to say that there may not have been better or identical examples elsewhere, it is just that the examples I have chosen (such as the Penistone line or the Newcastle & Carlisle Railway) are in some way or another representative of the point I am trying to make.

I hope you will enjoy this wander through time, the tangents I sometimes fly off to, and my personal interpretation of railway history. There are of course many views on any form of history, especially social history, but this is my attempt at providing an introduction to the subject from one particular standpoint. I hope it encourages you to look at the world the railways built in a different light.

Alan Earnshaw,
Appleby-in-Westmorland, July 2005

Below: *The railway companies very quickly came to realise that they needed to offer a comprehensive service to travellers, so they looked at ways of extending the railhead into the wider community. Almost every station had for example, a road delivery service to deliver and collect anything that was being sent by rail. This ranged from passengers luggage to all kinds of parcels and even heavy freight. They then began bus services, and even went into the shipping business. Many of Britain's ports were developed by the railways, first of all to handle freight (mainly coal), but then any kind of goods for import or export, along with items being sent to Ireland or other off-shore communities around the British coastline. One good example is Oban, seen here in 1948, sixty years after the railway arrived on this part of Scotland's west coast in 1888. The close association between the island ferries and the passenger station can easily be determined, but the railway also played a vital role in the carriage of goods into the town, whilst taking large quantities of fish back to Glasgow. British Railways*

THE ANCIENT APPLICATION OF RAILWAYS

The National Railway Museum's 'Railfest 2004' exhibition held in the Spring of 2004 was designed to celebrate 200 years of British railway history, taking the 1804 experiments of Richard Trevithick as a starting point.

However, the actual history is considerably older, and the antiquity probably dates back to the Middle Eastern civilisations of 4,000 years ago, so primitive British railways would have probably been quite familiar to the Babylonians, Egyptians, Persians and Phoenicians. In the ancient world primitive forms of railway existed on construction sites (such as the Pyramids of Egypt) and in mining areas (both underground and on the surface).

In various forms and guises they kept popping up through the centuries that followed, and were used wherever men needed to move heavy items from one place to another.

The Phoenicians, who were great travellers and explored the known world in search of ore mining areas with which they could trade, may well have helped export the technology of primitive railways in a piecemeal way. Yet, it was the Romans who brought with them the organised use of transport technology and expanded it throughout Europe. Their long straight roads are well known, but the story of their development of canals and guided road systems is less well understood. The Romans used canals primarily as a means of providing a water supply, but they did build canals that served as connections between navigable rivers.

Left: *The association between the horse and railway has long been recognised, but in some cases this kind of motive power is still employed. Take for example the short section of horse-drawn tramway that runs along the promenade at Douglas (on the Isle of Man) where horses are still in daily use.*

Top Right: *Although horses were widely used in the primitive railways, 'man-power' was used just as much, if not more. However, to push a wagon heavily loaded with either ore or coal was no easy matter, especially when the ground was rough. As a result miners developed planked 'ways' on which to push their loaded wagons, as seen here in this exhibit at the National Railway Museum, York.*

Bottom Right: *Discharging wagons such as the one seen above was no easy matter, but in the 17th century somebody came up with the idea of gravity discharge. Wagons, such as this Stockton & Darlington Railway 'chaldron wagon' show a design that was both simple and at the same time fitted into the 'coffin-shaped' levels constructed in the mines during the middle ages.*

The first of the canals thought to be built in Britain is the Fosse Dyke, which was constructed around 120 AD during the Roman occupation. This 11-mile (18km) long navigation connects the River Trent at Torksey to the River Witham at Lincoln, and is still in use today.

The guided roadway was more commonly used in mines and quarries, where they provided a link from the area of exploitation down to a navigable river or coastal port. Naturally, the development was limited and the application not especially intense, but in isolated ore-mining areas 'railways' or 'tramways' continued in use down to the 1600s. Thereafter, as coal began to supplant wood as a primary fuel, the use of these guided systems began to spread from the iron, lead and copper mines of the day, to the new coalfields that began to spring up; especially in Elizabethan England. In the 17th and 18th centuries the use of railways, plateways and waggonways continued to expand, but it was with the coming of the Industrial Revolution and the 19th century that they would provide the impetus for a rapid change from an agrarian society to an industrial one.

The way in which the railways affected not just the British Isles, but the world also, was staggering and from humble beginnings to the social changes that followed, the railways altered almost every aspect of life as we know it. This book charts those changes, and examines some of the key stages that occurred during this 200-year journey of technological advancement.

Above: *The reason for the first railways was not the carriage of passengers, but the movement of freight, predominantly coal. Although improvements were made over the 'chaldron' wagon, the British goods vehicle did not alter much for over a century and a half. Here we see a typical example of a mixed freight train behind Somerset & Dorset Joint Railway 7F 2-8-0 (53806) at Radstock on 16th April 1955. Note the variety of vehicles in the train as it heads towards Bath, with a 'banker' at the rear. Ivo Peters.*

THE ORIGINS OF RAIL

I am often asked, "where did railway technology begin, and who started it?", but these are questions that cannot be answered with any degree of historic satisfaction. We must therefore generalise, and leave readers to draw their own conclusions. It is safe to say that primitive railway systems and various types of railway engineering were around in ancient times, perhaps as long ago as 3,000 BC.

True there were no locomotives, and little in the form that we today would recognise as rolling stock, but the principle of wheeled transport being moved along rails or grooves was certainly evident in the ancient world. In his book *The Railways of Britain*, Professor Jack Simmons states: -

"The idea of a rail way – or a track, that is, constructed especially for the accommodation of wheeled vehicles – is to be found in Babylonia, Greece, and The Roman Empire. Wooden tracks, on which four-wheeled wagons ran, were in use in the mines of Germany, Alsace and Rumania in the 15th century."

Top Right: *A lead mine at Rookhope in the North Pennines during the 1890s showing a scene that would have been quite familiar to generations of miners in the same area.*

Bottom Right: *Although horse-haulage was quite common in the Pennine mines, hand 'tramming' of railway wagons was quite common in the smaller mines of the same orefield.*

The first primitive form of wheeled transport was the simple roller system, whereby using the boles of trees, early man learned that he could move heavy weights over a considerable distance. The Henge builders of the late Neolithic to early Bronze Age (that is 3,200-1,600BC), undoubtedly used tree trunks as rollers to move the large pieces of stone to the location where their monoliths were erected. Later the Vikings employed similar technology to haul their 'long boats' across land, especially when crossing an isthmus or avoiding waterfalls or rapids on a river. These were not railways as we know them, but the desire for technology was exactly the same: the need to move a heavy item from A to B, in the shortest possible time and also with the least possible effort. The technique was also employed on early construction sites in order to reduce friction, and we have evidence that sophisticated haulage and roller systems were employed in the construction of both the fabled city of Babylon and the Pyramids (two wonders of the ancient world). The Aztecs of Central America also employed a sort of sledge system on construction sites, but these sledges were pulled (usually by horses) along levelled ground between stones or timbers forming guide rails.

It was the introduction of the horse on these building sites, or for general haulage, that really influenced the development of the railways. Indeed the railway and the horse have long had a common affinity, and even today locomotives are still 'stabled' at the end of their day's activity. The horse-hauled cart also led to the development of the very first railway, or what we should more accurately describe as 'rut ways'. As the cart repeatedly trundled along its road, grooves were cut into the soil (or worn into the stone). It was further found that as long as these ruts remained dry, they were much easier to follow with the next cart and so on – a little like the principle of footsteps in the snow. Thus the first 'ways' were born, not by invention but by accident. In civilised areas, such as towns or cities, where roads were paved or metalled, these ruts soon wore grooves into the surface. Other than patch and repair these ruts, there was little that the waggoneers could do, but follow the lines left by their predecessors.

The Greeks certainly contributed to the development of rutways, and if they did not actively build them, they certainly perpetuated their continued use. Perhaps the classic example of a remaining rutway from the ancient world is that found at Syracuse, Sicily. There has been considerable debate about the development of rutways on the main Roman highways, and frankly there is little evidence to suggest that these ever developed significantly on the long distance routes. However, this does not preclude the fact that such rutways would develop on intensely used routes, such as those leading to and from sea ports or industrial sites like quarries and mines. At a variety of places around the Mediterranean Sea, there is ample evidence of the way in which rutways developed, and how things like standard gauges, crossing points, passing loops, sidings and (above all) reasonably level gradients were formed.

The railways thus owe their standard gauge to the Romans (or even earlier Middle Eastern civilisation), but much more was to be copied by the railway builders of the 19th century. For instance Roman architecture, with its many graceful structures, contributed much, including the aqueduct. Built to carry watercourses across ravines and valleys, and at the same time maintain a level plane, aqueducts were ideal models for the railway builders. With their tall piers, graceful curved arches and apparently spindly construction (which actually attained great structural strength), the aqueduct was the perfect solution for the early railway builders. In tunnelling, embanking and cutting procedures, the railway engineers also borrowed from the ancient world, adapting what had gone before for that which was yet to come.

Many writers on railway subjects have suggested that railways, or more accurately tramways, first originated in the coalfields of northern England. It was here that Elizabeth's father (Henry VIII) had dissolved the Catholic monasteries and faced the potentially serious Northern Uprisings or rebellions. His daughter, to re-settle the land and quell rebellion, gave grants of huge tracts of land to a new class of Protestant noblemen, and ironically it was on these lands that large deposits of coal were later found. However, it is not strictly true to claim that the railways are a product of the North East! Although the first recorded use of railways does indeed span back to this era, it is at Woolaton, Nottinghamshire that we find the first accurately recorded date of their use (1604), whilst the first railway authorised by an Act of Parliament dates to 1712 and the Middleton Railway in Yorkshire. However, it can be reasonably suggested that the Northumberland and Durham mine-owners (who began developing their operations in the Elizabethan-era) had borrowed a form of technology from the lead mines of the North Pennines, which were located a few miles to the west. In these mines, which had been operated in Roman, Saxon and Norman times, primitive railways were to be found in both the underground galleries and between the mine heads and the crushing or smelting plants. Given the heavy nature of lead ore (galena), it is reasonable to think that the easiest and smoothest means of transport would have been employed. It is also reasonable to suggest that the 'standard gauge' railway would have its origins here too.

In Roman times, the authorities had set Imperial Standards for almost everything, and horse-drawn carts were by no means exempt from this. The 'standard' for a horse-drawn 'draught' cart was five foot (1.527m) across the shafts; in turn this meant that the in-line wheels of the cart would leave ruts of four feet eight inches (1.425m) on the ground. On this point *The Oxford Companion to British Railway History* states "Horse-drawn vehicles have throughout history commonly been built with their wheels 5 feet apart because this suits the proportions of the horse. There is some evidence that grooved stones were used for guidance on trackways built for bulk horse-drawn transport, from which early railways and tramroads developed. Thus, when rails replaced the grooved stones, it was natural that the distance between them should be about 4' 8"."

It was no accident then that the gauge for many of the mine waggonways in Northern England was four feet eight-and-a-half inches (1.425m). Nor that the final standardisation on this gauge by Stephenson took place on Lord Carlisle's Waggonway, which ran on the boundary between the coal mining and lead mining areas and within the North Pennines. (Ironically, it would be to this very same waggonway that Stephenson's *Rocket* would be sent to eke out its day following its unsuccessful working life on the Liverpool & Manchester Railway.)

The new coal-mining operations were extremely profitable but they were dependent on the sale of their produce to towns and cities. London and a few other major communities were the predominant market place, and therefore the transportation of this 'black gold' had to be arranged! The old waggonways and tramways used within the mines were extended down to a point on a navigable river, and the coal trans-shipped into keel boats. These boats would take the coal further down the shallow rivers to a point where coasting vessels could anchor, and further trans-shipment took place before the coal was exported southwards. In the Midlands, coal was taken into the fast-growing 'potteries' of Staffordshire, where bottle kilns belched out their dark smoky fumes.

Top Right: *The use of inclines, both those that were self-acting and those that were powered by winding engines, were part of the philosophy of early engineers. This winding engine at Crawley Bank Top on the Stanhope & Tyne Railroad (which opened in 1834), shows the principle of drawing trucks by a fixed engine to good effect.*

Bottom Right: *The self-acting inclines were only useful where the bulk of traffic had to descend from a higher altitude; as seen in this 65-chain long example at Ingleby on the Rosedale Ironstone Railway that opened in 1858. The two-rail principle can be seen in the photograph, and the general steepness (as great as 1 in 5 in places) can be appreciated.*

Elsewhere, the 'Black Country' became aptly named due to the polluting effects of industrialisation. The coalfields of West Yorkshire fed the growing mill towns of the old West Riding and those in Lancashire did the same for the cotton-producing factories. Meanwhile the North Eastern rivers of Tyne, Wear and Tees are classic examples of how extensive the export of coal became, but the activity on the River Severn or the ports of South Wales also provide further examples to show how widespread this trade was.

Of course, many early railways were just primarily intended as 'feeders' for canals, navigable rivers and coastal shipping, but there were quite a number of land-locked areas that could not be served by sailing vessels. The transport system that existed at that time was merely a collection of winding, un-surfaced mud roads linking village to village, although some of the old Roman roads remained in use and a limited system of surfaced toll roads had been built. Canals, and the barges they carried, proved more than adequate for unlocking the terrain not served by navigable rivers. So new waterways were constructed to link areas of mineral exploitation to manufacturing districts, and manufacturing districts to places where the goods were consumed or exported.

Top Left: *The concept of manufactured goods or raw materials being shipped to other areas or overseas can be seen in microcosm around the Severn Valley. This is especially so at Ironbridge, where the industrial revolution can be understood in a distinct number of ways through a collection of museums. A visit is highly recommended, as it will clearly illustrate how the components of the industrial revolution all came together.*

Bottom Left: *Two types of canal developed in the industrial era, the broad canal (with lock widths of 14 feet) and the narrow canal (with lock widths of seven feet). However, this meant that goods had to be frequently transhipped from one kind of barge to another, as here at the junction of the Sir John Ramsden Canal (1776) and the Huddersfield Narrow Canal (1811).*

The Ironbridge World Heritage Site near Telford in Shropshire provides a great introduction to the subject of industrialisation and 18th century technical progress, but its development was not altogether unique in Britain at that time. All over the land vast mineral reserves (such as coal and iron ore) and natural resources (such as timber) were being exploited to create huge quantities of manufactured goods. All of this movement of raw materials and finished goods required transportation, and the quicker the goods could be got to market (either at home or overseas), the cheaper they became.

Thus the goods sold in greater quantities and this then made greater profits for the manufacturers, who in turn invested more money to find better ways of making their goods or mechanising the process. The better methods of iron production that Abraham Darby developed at Ironbridge were one of the major catalysts, but improved transport was the crux of the matter, as industrialists needed to overcome the restrictions of coastal shipping or river transport and find an alternative to the horses and carts that could only carry one or two tons of cargo at a time.

THE CANAL ERA AND BEYOND

The canal network increased massively during the 18th and early-19th centuries as the demand for industrial transport increased, and an inland transport network rapidly developed. Highways of that time were still unsuitable for any volume of traffic, as road vehicles were unable to transport large amounts of materials quickly. The new canal system demonstrated an economic and reliable way to transport goods and commodities in large quantities, but for many it was either too slow or in the wrong place. Their biggest problem was that the canals needed to be completely level, and even minor rises or falls in elevation had to be overcome by long sweeping deviations or the construction of 'locks', which enabled the canal boat to ascend or descend.

Above: *To move heavy goods a long distance, a smooth surface was needed to take the place of horse and carts, which at best could move around three tons at about six miles per hour on the poor roads of the 18th century. To find out how one horse could effortlessly pull a heavy load, why not try a horse-drawn barge trip along the Llangollen Canal?*

Canal development was one way to improve the poor roads of the period, which would become un-usable after heavy rain. Because of the small loads that could be carried, supply of essential commodities such as coal, iron ore, wool and cotton was limited, and this kept prices high, and restricted economic growth. Although the canals were very costly to build, they were ideal for wealthy men like the Third Earl of Bridgewater, who owned a number of coal mines in northern England.

Top Left: *The Huddersfield Narrow Canal was 19 3/4 miles (32km) long including the world's longest canal tunnel at Standedge (three miles 135 yards or 4,950m), which was later extended by a further 283 yards. It was abandoned by the LMS railway (following an Act of Parliament) in 1941, but is seen here at the western portal in 1951.* The late David Ibbotson

Bottom Left: *The eastern end at Standedge, in the 1960s long after abandonment of the canal. Note the close proximity of the railway lines.* The late Eric Treacy

By the middle of the 18th century, the Duke found that he needed a reliable way to get his coal to the rapidly industrialising city of Manchester, so he commissioned the engineer James Brindley to build a canal. The resulting Bridgewater Canal opened in 1761 and was the first canal of the modern era to be built in Britain. The boats (barges) used on the canal were horse-drawn as a 'tow-path' was built alongside the canal for the horse to use, and this method of operation proved to be highly economical. It would become standard across the British canal network and commercial horse-drawn canal boats could be seen on Britain's canals until the 1950s.

With only one horse pulling a boat, 30-tons could be transported at a time; this being more than ten times the amount of cargo a horse could move with a cart. Because of this huge increase in supply, the Bridgewater canal reduced the cost of coal in Manchester to one third of its original price within just a year of opening. The canal was such a huge financial success that it had repaid the cost of its construction within just a few years.

This success hinted at the viability of canal transport, and industrialists in many other parts of the country soon wanted canals. Within just a few years of the Bridgewater's opening, an embryonic national canal network came into being, with the construction of waterways in many parts of Britain.

To keep down building costs, some canals were built to a narrow width; the standard dimension of canal locks introduced by Brindley in 1766 were 72' 7" inches (22.1m) long by 7' 6" (2.3m) wide. This restricted the size of the boats and thus limited the quantity of the cargo they could carry to around 30 tons. This decision would in later years make the canal system economically un-viable for freight transport, because by the mid-20th century it was no longer possible to work a 30-ton load economically.

The period between the 1770s and the 1830s is often referred to as the 'Golden Age' of the canal. During this period of 'canal mania', huge sums were invested in new routes, and the canal system rapidly expanded to nearly 4,000 miles (7,000km) in length, and essentially had no competition from other forms of transport. Many different rival canal companies were formed, often competing bitterly. The end result of this competition saw both a reduction of carriage costs and the expansion of the canal system, which in turn dramatically speeded up industrialisation across Britain.

The trouble with the canal system was the fact that it was a very fixed infrastructure and not readily adaptable for the emerging industrial needs. For example branches from the main routes were difficult and expensive to construct, so railways or waggonways had to be built to provide links into the system. This in turn resulted in the costly and time-consuming process of transhipping loads between tramway and canal!

Top Right: *Interest in canals re-emerged after World War II, but as a means of leisure and not as a freight carrier. In 1952 a group of enthusiasts explore the disused Standedge Tunnel.*

Bottom Right *The Leeds & Liverpool Canal was a very circuitous route and as goods took a long time to deliver, the financiers' returns on their investment were very slow. Conversely, by the 1970s the route was just perfect for use by pleasure craft such as these seen in Skipton.*

Top Left: *A section of original plateway used at Coalbrookdale and now preserved in the local museum. Note how the cast-iron 'rails' were of a 'U' section, and that the wheels of the waggon ran in the central channel, as cross members held the track together.*

Bottom Left: *A handbill advertising the Surrey Iron Railway, and showing how the practice of publishing rates and tariffs came about. It is interesting that this notice is dated 1804, around the time when Trevithick was doing his early experiments on the Pen-y-Darren Tramway in Wales. The railway from Wandsworth Basin to Croydon did not remain horse-operated for long and eventually became part of a steam railway, but it is interesting to speculate just how far this early kind of tramway might have developed, had the Napoleonic Wars not forced up the price of horse fodder?*

By this stage manufacturers, seeking to speed up their delivery of goods to the market, were naturally asking, why not create a tramway that could take the goods all the way to the market concerned. The answer, during the 18th century was entirely dependent on the question of motive power, and as long as horses remained the prime-movers, the plate ways and waggon ways (with their uneven formations) did not provide a credible alternative.

Take for example the World's first 'public railway', the eight-and-a-quarter mile long Surrey Iron Railway, which opened to horse-drawn traffic in 1805 following the Act of Parliament of 1801 that had authorised its construction. It ran from Wandsworth on the River Thames, serving mills in the Wandle Valley before terminating at Croydon. Engineered by William Jessop, it employed a four foot two-and-a-half inch gauge, using stone sleepers and 'L-shaped' rails in three foot long sections.

By 1802 its promoters had set their sights on a railway connecting London to Portsmouth, which in turn would incorporate the Croydon Merstham & Goldstone Iron Railway. It made significant contributions to the developments that followed, and it rested the initiative from the canal owners who primarily saw all railways as 'feeders' to their system. The canal 'tramways' would include significant examples such as the Little Eaton Gangroad in Derbyshire, the Loughborough & Nanpantan or the complex network of canal lines in South Wales. On this subject *The Oxford Companion To British Railway History* states, "the early iron-railways saw the piecemeal adoption of most of the ingredients that finally came together to create the 'modern' railway. The Stockton & Darlington was the last to be built in this formative period of railway history; the Liverpool & Manchester of 1830 was, for all practical purposes, the first representative of the Railway Age".

So, it was in the north eastern coalfield that the biggest improvements and technology seemed to spring forward, as one form of technology was worked to its final extent and then moved on to something bigger and better. This shift from early railway technology to the kind applied by Stephenson on the Liverpool & Manchester was not however a product of North West England, but of the North Eastern counties, especially after the mines on the coastal fringe became 'worked out' and newer ones were opened further inland. As the distances from the coal mines to the navigable ports became longer. The longer the distance that coal needed transporting, the better methods of traction were required, especially when hand-tramming and horse-power were not able to meet up to the rigours of the work.

The advent of the Napoleonic war co-incided with this move inland and impacted severely on horse haulage, especially as the price of fodder escalated and eventually became rationed. Consequently, various examples of 'mechanical horses' were tried over the years, and between 1804 and 1824 a whole range of experiments were tried. These varied from Trevithick's experiments, to those of Matthew Murray (Middleton Railway), who experimented with rack and pinion drive to help show that steel wheels could be run successfully on steel rails. Other engineers, such as Hedley, Stephenson and Hackworth all strove to show that railways could be operated by steam engines working on the 'adhesion-only' principle. From Trevithick through to *Locomotion*, many schemes came and went as will be told in a forthcoming book in this series.

Above: *Early steam railway experiments were plagued by track, wheel and axle failures, and these are demonstrated by the replica of Trevithick's Penydarren engine (1804), which broke an axle whilst taking part in the National Railway Museum's Railfest (200 Years of Rail) celebrations in the spring of 2004.*

On the Stockton & Darlington Railway, Stephenson recruited Timothy Hackworth, one of the engineers who had helped William Hedley on *Puffing Billy*. Their first railway locomotive, *Locomotion*, was finished in September 1825. It was similar to those that Stephenson had produced at the Tyneside collieries, but the boiler of the *Locomotion* had a single fire tube and two vertical cylinders let into the barrel and the four wheels that were coupled by rods, rather than a chain.

THE STEAM RAILWAY ARRIVES

Stephenson's engine *Locomotion* inaugurated services on the world's first 'public steam railway', which opened in County Durham in 1825. When this line, the Stockton & Darlington, opened it successfully reduced the cost of transporting coal from 18 shillings per ton to eight-shillings and sixpence per ton, and it soon became clear that large profits could be made by building railways. Railways therefore showed that a line of cheap communication could be opened between coastal ports and their hinterland, and soon a series of schemes were being promulgated all over Britain. Among these early ideas we find that a canal, which was being proposed between Newcastle & Carlisle was dropped in favour of a railway, whilst another embryonic plan envisaged taking a horse-operated railway inland from the small port of Whitby on the east coast to the inland market town of Pickering.

Above: *Stephenson's* Locomotion *made world history in 1825, and 150 years later its replica was found back on the course of the former Stockton & Darlington Railway during the celebrations of 1975. The replica is seen in charge of a short train including a chaldron wagon and an original S&DR coach.*

This involved a route of 24 miles, much of which crossed the bleak and lonely North Yorkshire Moors, and was built many years ahead of railway proposals for the bustling port of Hull further down the East Yorkshire coast. George Stephenson was at the heart of many of these schemes, and in the North West, a group of businessmen led by James Sandars recruited him to build their Liverpool & Manchester Railway. This scheme had been proposed in 1821 in order to create a railway to reduce the costs of transporting raw materials and finished goods between Manchester (the centre of the textile industry) and Liverpool (the most important port in the north of England).

Top Right: *The world's oldest preserved locomotive* Puffing Billy *designed by William Hedley for the Wylam Colliery in 1813 regularly worked trains of 50-tons at between four and five mph for 48-years (although it was extensively modified throughout its working life). It was 'loaned' to the Patent Office Museum, London (the forerunner of the Science Museum) in 1862.*

Centre Right: *The Hetton Colliery in Co. Durham was a completely new mine, which opened in 1822 and it was planned to use steam locomotives to haul the coal to the newly erected staithes on the River Wear near Sunderland. The Hetton locomotives were much modified over the ensuing years, this one lasted to be preserved in York's Queen Street Railway Museum.*

Bottom Right: *Following its withdrawal on Lord Carlisle's waggonway in the North Pennines, Stephenson's* Rocket *was rescued by the Science Museum. Here we see what are unkindly called the 'Rocket Remains' on display in the 1960s.*

The Liverpool & Manchester initially engaged William James, who promised to build the line in 18-months for £100,000, but little progress was made. Stephenson replaced James in 1824 and was assisted by Allcard, Dixon and Locke. However, when it came to the Parliamentary enquiry, Stephenson failed to answer questions put to him in the Parliamentary hearings. As a result the plans were thrown out due to inaccurate measurements and Stephenson was then fired by the Board. He was replaced by John and George Rennie and their assistant Charles Blacker Vignoles, and in 1826 Parliament gave permission for the railway to be built. Stephenson was then re-appointed as engineer to oversee the construction, but he was faced with a large number of engineering problems; including crossing the unstable peat bog at Chat Moss, a nine-arched viaduct across the Sankey Valley and a two-mile long rock cutting at Olive Mount.

The resulting railway was 31 miles long and consisted of a double line of rails of the fish-bellied type and laid on stone or timber sleepers. Passenger trains started at the Crown Street Station in Liverpool and after passing the Moorish Arch at Edge Hill terminated at Water Street in Manchester.

However, the directors of the Liverpool & Manchester company were still unsure whether to use locomotives or stationary engines on their line. To help them reach a decision, it was decided to hold a competition at Rainhill in 1829 where the winning locomotive would be awarded £500. The idea being that if the locomotive was good enough, it would be the one used on the new railway.

Top Left: We have postulated that railways of a kind were known in the Stone Age, but stone certainly lasted into the Railway Age, especially on early lines like the Stanhope & Tyne. It was used there as a basic building material for a variety of purposes. Obviously buildings and bridges were prime examples, but here they have been used for boundary stones, as the line was built without an Act of Parliament; this one near Waskerley, Co. Durham marked the extent of the railway land.

Centre & Bottom Left: What at first looks to be a stone wall near Waskerley, is in fact a very significant piece of the railway's 'stone-age' technology. These are the old sleeper blocks on which the Stanhope & Tyne Railroad was laid when it opened in 1834. A close-up view in the lower picture clearly shows where the chairs were fitted directly on to the stone sleeper blocks. Few cross-ties were used, as the weight of the blocks kept the track in place.

As history records, the winner of that trial was the now world-famous *Rocket*, which demonstrated the dual-efficiency of a locomotive with inclined pistons and a multi-tubed boiler; and with this locomotive the Liverpool & Manchester railway opened on 15th September 1830. The Prime Minister, the Duke of Wellington, and a large number of important people had attended the opening ceremony that included a procession of eight locomotives, including the *Northumbrian*, the *Rocket*, the *North Star* and the *Phoenix*.

The Liverpool & Manchester railway was a great success, and not just for freight; for in 1831 the company transported no less than 445,047 passengers. Receipts were £155,702 with profits of £71,098. By 1844 receipts had reached £258,892 with profits of £136,688. During this period, the shareholders were regularly paid out an annual dividend of £10 for every £100 invested. Stephenson became a national hero, and it seemed that every town wanted his advice on how to construct a railway. Just a few of those might be quoted as examples, as these show the versatility and widespread nature of his projects: -

Canterbury & Whitstable 1830
Leicester & Swanington 1832
Stanhope & Tyne 1834
Whitby & Pickering 1836
Grand Junction Railway 1837
London & Birmingham Railway 1837-8
Newcastle & Carlisle 1839
Manchester & Leeds Railway 1840
Maryport & Carlisle 1840
Lancaster & Carlisle 1846

However, of all the early railways, the London & Birmingham may well be said to be the most consequential of all. After the success of the Liverpool & Manchester Railway, people in Birmingham began to consider having a railway to their city. It had seen rapid economic growth in the 1820s and by 1830 was sending one thousand tons of goods every week to London by canal. It was therefore decided to approach George Stephenson, the chief engineer of the Liverpool & Manchester line, about the possibility of building a railway between Birmingham and London. Stephenson advised them about the route that the railway should take but suggested that his son Robert become the chief engineer. Many people living on the proposed route were bitterly opposed to the railway; for example, the landowners of Northampton forced Stephenson to make the line pass some distance from their town. As a result of this change, Stephenson had to build a 2,400-yard long tunnel at Kilsby. Another major engineering problem that faced Stephenson was the Blisworth Cutting.

Top Right: The 112-mile long London to Birmingham line took 20,000 men nearly five years to build and at a total cost of £5,500,000 (approximately £50,000 a mile). The railway was opened in stages and finally completed on 17th September 1838. The line started at Euston Station in London and finished at Curzon Street Station in Birmingham, where railways to other parts of the country were already built or in the course of construction. As the Grand Junction Railway had been finished in July 1837, it provided a route north to Earlestown on the Liverpool & Manchester; thus the four major cities in England (London, Birmingham, Manchester and Liverpool) were all linked together. Needless to say that Stephenson (assisted by Locke) had also been behind this scheme as well. This original lithograph by Bourne shows work progressing on Watford Tunnel in 1837.

Centre Right: Another image by Bourne that shows the construction period, reveals a scene at Camden where work on the engine houses and the winding engine is underway. The scope of engineering on the London & Birmingham Railway was quite considerable, especially when it was still in the time of the primitive railway. For instance, at the time it was opened, engines could not operate down to the terminus at Euston, and a winding engine was needed to haul carriages up and down the incline.

Bottom Right: Fortunately, the incline was later replaced by adhesion operation, as is seen by Jubilee Class 4-6-0 Leinster passing Camden No. 2 Box in the early 1950s. British Railways

Top Left: *Originally constructed for an American railway to five foot six inch gauge, the* North Star *was altered to suit the GWR's seven foot-and-a-quarter inch gauge when the sale fell through. It was shipped to Maidenhead by barge at the end of 1837 and remained there until the rails reached that area in May 1838.*

Centre Left: *Unlike Stephenson's gauge of four foot eight-and-a-half inches, Brunel's 'broad gauge' required much more land and was costly to construct. Despite the greater level of safety, with more stable engines (like this 0-6-0), the difference between the two gauges would plague the exchange of railway traffic until the last of the Broad Gauge system was finally abandoned in 1892.*

Bottom Left: *On Saturday 21st May 1892 over 4,200 platelayers and gangers were assembled along the GWR main line ready to undertake conversion from the broad gauge. All the rolling stock and non-essential engines had been worked to Swindon, whereby at mid-day on Saturday 15 miles of specially prepared temporary sidings were filled with a collection of rolling stock and locomotives that would never be seen again. This collection of redundant locomotives would have included 0-6-0ST 1280.*

One of Stephenson's contemporaries, whose name will forever be linked with the early railways, was Isambard Kingdom Brunel. He joined the Great Western Railway (GWR) on 7th March 1833, as the engineer engaged to build a railway between Bristol and London. He was no stranger to Bristol, as he had already built the Clifton Suspension Bridge and seen his plans for harbour improvements accepted. By August 1833 he had produced his plans for the railway and the estimated cost was £2,805,330. It took two years of a long hard argument, but on 31st August 1835 the Bill for "the line laid down by Mr. Brunel" from Bristol to London with stations at Bath, Chippenham, Swindon, Maidenhead and Reading with branch lines to Trowbridge and Bradford-on-Avon received the Royal Assent.

The railway was 118 miles long and it took six years to build. The hardest part was the two-mile long tunnel at Box between Bath and Chippenham, which took five-years to dig, a whole year longer than had been planned. On 30th June 1841 the directors of the GWR left London and made the first train journey to Bristol in four hours. During the next 20 years the GWR expanded so quickly that, by the 1860s, it covered almost the same area as it did 100 years later. It reached Weymouth in the south, most of Devon and Cornwall, South Wales as well as reaching into Birmingham and the Midlands with a line through Cheltenham and Gloucester from Swindon.

The period from the 1840s to the 1890s saw intense railway building activity, often with rival lines being promoted along parallel routes and into towns where several railway companies erected their own stations. For example, the small textile-manufacturing town of Dewsbury in West Yorkshire had four separate railways and stations, these being the London & North Western Railway, The Great Northern Railway, The Lancashire & Yorkshire Railway, and the Midland Railway. However, the latter company's services came so late, that their through route was abandoned beyond Dewsbury after World War I and with them went the plans for a grand station building; even so huge goods warehouses were built and extensively used. So it was that a period of rivalry, competing routes and services developed, as the Victorians shunned any form of monopoly. In some places, Parliament did ensure that joint schemes were developed, and places like Huddersfield (another Yorkshire woollen mill town, and just a few miles from Dewsbury) saw the construction of a joint passenger station shared mainly by the L&YR and LNWR, but also accommodating trains from the Great Central, the Midland and the Great Northern railways.

Above: *The mania of the 1840s saw little evidence of co-operation between any of the early railway companies, but having involved himself with the North Midland Railway, George Hudson saw it as part of a dream he had for a grand trunk railway running from London to Scotland. Here we see a Midland Railway 2-4-0 locomotive by Kirtley, built for its main line express services.*

Yet, in the period when the issue of free enterprise waged war with state control, one man stands out completely above the rest. Some think he was a charlatan, others a 'con-man', yet others say he was merely an opportunist who saw an emerging market and found a way to monopolise it. At the time he was hailed as a hero, made a city leader, elected a Member of Parliament and became known as the Railway King. He was certainly a visionary, and he had the foresight of seeing the need for inter-connecting railway systems and the amalgamation of what were otherwise purely local schemes, turning them into enterprises that were of national benefit. This man was George Hudson, the son of a farmer, who was born at Howsham in the Yorkshire Wolds in March 1800.

After a local education Hudson became an apprentice draper in York, but he impressed his employers so much that he eventually became a partner in the business. In turn he took an interest in both local politics and the York Union Bank. Purely by chance, the latter was then actively assisting Glyn's Bank of London in the financing of the London & Birmingham line.

By another co-incidence, Hudson then happened to be in Whitby in 1834 inspecting some property that he had been left, when he met George Stephenson who had gone there in connection with the planned Whitby & Pickering Railway. The book *The Railway King* written by Lambert in 1934 states: -

"It was indeed at a curiously opportune moment that these two so dissimilar, yet complementary, geniuses had come together. For in 1834 the English railway system was about to experience one of its periodic spasms of feverish expansions; the country was on the eve of an outburst of railway speculation. The first of these outbursts had taken place after the successful opening of the Stockton and Darlington in 1825; ten years passed, with a trough of disillusionment and stagnation, and a second and higher wave of speculation rose in 1835; and finally, there was yet to come the third and greatest - the 'Railway Mania' of 1845.

On each occasion the same symptoms were repeated - an increase of optimism concerning the future of railways, a sudden maturing of schemes, and then a ruthless elimination, by competition, of the weakest or 'less fit' of these schemes, leaving a residuum of additions to the country's railway mileage. The belated opening in 1830 of the Liverpool and Manchester Railway was almost the only substantial fruit of the initial outburst of enterprise in 1825; and thereafter, on the strength of the prestige which he had gained there, George Stephenson interested himself in schemes for short lengths of line in the Midlands, designed as links in a great chain of communication between north and south.

To Stephenson it seemed axiomatic that the main railway artery from London to the north should run through the Midlands into Lancashire or Yorkshire; for such an artery would connect up the principal pre-railway centres of industry - pottery, hardware, coal, and textiles. Consequently as soon as the London and Birmingham Railway was begun, he started planning a trunk route running from Rugby or Birmingham up to his own home city, Newcastle, ultimately to continue along the east coast into Scotland. It was a grand conception - and to carry it out Stephenson began to build railways through the Midlands up to Leeds, but Hudson led him to change his plan and make York, not Leeds, the pivot of his north-eastern route."

Yet many still envisaged the idea of a horse-drawn railway and they used the support of the great engineer James Rennie, but Stephenson persuaded the York speculators that this would not be in their best interests. Hudson then made his famous comment "mak all t'railways cum t'York"; suggesting that the city should become the primary centre (or hub) for all the steam-operated railways in eastern England. In 1827 a relative had left Hudson £30,000 in his will and he subsequently decided to use the money to promote a line from York to connect (at Normanton) with Stephenson's North Midland Railway from Derby to Leeds. After raising £446,000 the York & North Midland Railway was completed on 29th May 1839.

Not content with a link to London (albeit circuitous), his next enterprise was to invest in the Great North of England Company, so that they could complete their line to Newcastle-upon-Tyne. To obtain permission from the House of Commons, Hudson is alleged to have distributed over £3,000 in bribes. Hudson followed this by joining the Midland Railway Company, for which he raised the sum of £5,000,000 to allow further expansion. To persuade people to invest in the company he personally guaranteed the payment of a six per cent dividend.

Hudson was also active in politics and for many years he was the leader of the Conservative Party in York and he held a series of positions in the city including Councillor (1835), Alderman (1836) and Lord Mayor (1837). He was asked to stand as the Member of Parliament for Whitby, and he had a good standing in the town due to his involvement with the local railways, as well as having many land-holdings in the area.

However, it was his business interests in Sunderland, where he also supported both the docks and the railways, that enabled him to be elected as Conservative MP for the town in the General Election of 1845. Once elected to the House of Commons, Hudson argued strongly against any suggestions that the railway system should come under government (state) supervision. His line from York to the Tyne opened in 1844 after a number of problems, but this meant that Hudson's companies now controlled 1,016 miles of railway track.

As stated before, he obtained the title 'The Railway King' as a result, and many new railway companies actively sought his involvement or advice. A survey in 1845 revealed that Hudson had already invested £319,835 in railway shares, but even so he continued to buy shares in new and existing railway companies. He also purchased a controlling interest in the Newcastle & North Shields Railway and the Great North of England Railway, but it was later revealed that some of his share-dealings were not being entered in the company's account books.

Top Right: As the age of the train dawned upon the British Isles, railways were built all across the land with both passenger and freight schemes being put forward. This example here shows an extension of the Weardale Iron Company's railway being built in the late-19th century. The engine is a Joicey 0-4-0ST, which was later converted to an 0-6-0ST.

Centre Right: The curving sweep of Thomas Bouch's Tay Bridge during construction. This tall, spindly edifice replaced a train ferry that had previously traversed the Firth, and a similar bridge was planned for the Firth of Forth until disaster struck Tayside in 1879.

Bottom Right: Many railway constructors used their own locomotives as part of the track-building work. This Manning Wardle 0-4-0 tank engine is typical of the period. Naylor Brothers

George Hudson became a close friend of George Stephenson and they went into partnership together, opening collieries, ironworks and limestone quarries in the Chesterfield area. Stephenson also agreed to join the board of the York & North Midland line in 1840. However, five years later he had become suspicious of Hudson's methods and resigned. He confided his reasons in a letter to Michael Longridge (his partner in the Robert Stephenson & Co locomotive business) on 22nd November 1845, stating: -

"Hudson has become too great a man for me now. I am not at all satisfied at the way the Newcastle and Berwick line has been carried on and I do not intend to take any more active part in it. I have made Hudson a rich man but he will very soon care for nobody except he can get money by them. I make these observations in confidence to you."

Hudson had also developed a close friendship with the Duke of Wellington, who was not only the hero of the Napoleonic Wars but then became the Prime Minister. Hudson helped Wellington to make a great deal of money by advising him on when to buy and sell railway shares. When Wellington asked Hudson what he could do in return, the Railway King simply asked him to visit his daughter at her expensive private school in Hampstead as many of the girls had been making fun at Hudson's social background, and he wanted Wellington to increase her status in the school.

Hudson was also a generous man and entertained lavishly, and seemingly not just for show as he did a great deal for those who he considered to be his inferiors. However, what he did do was a little practice that we would now call 'insider-dealing', using privileged information to manipulate share prices.

In the short-term this made Hudson and his friends a great deal of money, but railway shares became over-priced and their value began to fall dramatically towards the end of 1847. People who had heavily invested in railway share dealing faced financial ruin, and not unnaturally a great deal of hostility was turned on the man who had persuaded them to buy shares. Systematically Hudson was forced to resign as chairman of all the railway companies under his control, even his beloved York & North Midland.

A committee of investigation was formed to look into Hudson's railway companies and it soon became clear to them that he had not always told potential share-buyers the truth about the real financial state of his companies. The investigators also alleged that Hudson had been paying bribes to MPs. They said Hudson had also sold shares and land to both the Great North and Newcastle & Berwick railways at inflated prices. He did not dispute these offences and agreed to pay back the money he had 'swindled' from the shareholders. Despite this admission of corruption, Hudson was able to remain as MP for Sunderland until 1859.

However, he could not pay back the money he owed to shareholders and in July 1865, he was imprisoned in York Castle for debt. After his remaining friends raised a substantial sum of money to pay off these debts, Hudson was released in October 1866. For many the case was still not proven against the Railway King, and he was well received in both Sunderland and Whitby after his discharge from prison. In his life, he must have seen the progress that his inspired vision (whether it was motivated by greed, incompetence or over-enthusiasm) had taken the railways of Britain all over the country. Few of the great lines were left to build when George Hudson died on 14th December 1871, and despite the many charges levelled against him, he must have been content with seeing just how much the country's transport infrastructure had developed during the 37 years since he had first met George Stephenson.

Top Left: *A portrait of George Stephenson 'The Father Of The Railways', who as a self-taught man took the new form of traction to unheard of levels of success. His determination and drive, when coupled with the ambitious nature of George Hudson led to the North East of England becoming the 'cradle of the railways'.*

Bottom Left: *Near York railway station there stands a statue of George Leeman, the arch-enemy of George Hudson (seen left), who assumed the mantle of the 'Railway King' when he was disgraced.. The crowning insult for Hudson was the fact that the statue (which had been modelled before his fall from grace), was re-modelled and given Leeman's head instead.*

MOVING ON FROM THE MANIA

After the periods of railway mania, Britain's railway map was largely drawn and thereafter the operating companies needed to consolidate and improve their services. Many criticisms of train working arrangements are recorded in this period, as for example Mirfield, where the railway provided a billiard table to help passengers pass the time whilst waiting for trains. Clearly, any money spent had to go on improving the system and had to be used on a more efficient means of operating. Doubling or even quadrupling schemes were implemented, the long single-line tunnels below hills like the Pennines were given a second bore running alongside (as at Woodhead and Standedge), whilst curves were straightened out to prove smoother running.

Above: *The movement of coal by rail remained vital to the economy of South Wales from the days of Trevithick down to the time Margaret Thatcher systematically demolished both industries! Here ex-Rhymney Railway 0-6-2T 42 (GWR 38) heads under Walnut Tree Viaduct in September 1957.* R. O. Tuck

Visually, the biggest area of improvement was in the field of bridge construction, which has to be said was much-needed on some lines. Many of the early railways had employed tall, spindly bridges and viaducts, some of which were timber trestles that would not look out of place in a film about the American Wild West. For instance, Brunel was a great advocate of timber viaducts, and those that he built on the route down to Cornwall were amongst some of his greatest works of civil engineering.

Left: *In my book on the history of Cowans Sheldon, I inadvertently captioned this as the Beelah Viaduct on the Stainmore line. It is in fact Deepdale, another of Thomas Bouch's tall, spindly cast-iron viaducts. Located between Lartington and Bowes, it was erected in 1861 and was 740 feet long, 161 feet above the bed of the river and 24 feet between the parapets. It had 11 spans, each of 60 feet and cost the (then) staggering sum of £20,687. Opened in 1861, the Stainmore line lasted just over 100 years, closing in 1962. Yet despite the problems with Bouch's Tay Bridge, the viaducts on the Stainmore line withstood all that the Pennine weather could throw at them.*

The public were far from sure about these wooden creations, especially those that creaked and groaned as trains passed over them, or those that swayed alarmingly during strong winds. Tall railway bridges had been known in Britain for some time, and the one built on the waggonway at Causey Arch in County Durham in 1727 had the largest span of all at 105 feet. Another early example was Laigh Milton Viaduct of 1812, which was found on the Kilmarnock & Troon Railway. Two timber viaducts built on Tyneside, at Ouseburn and Willington, caused so much concern that they were later replaced by iron structures. Timber viaducts on the Lancashire & Yorkshire Railway (at Denby Dale, Horbury and Mytholm Bridge) caused so much concern that public petitions were raised to bring about their replacement. George Stephenson was asked to write a report into their safety and although he pronounced the spans to be structurally sound, the destruction of Horbury Viaduct by fire did little to inspire public confidence.

Yet, it was in Scotland where public confidence in viaducts took their major blow, and did so in more ways than one. During a savage storm on 28th December 1879, the high girders of Sir Thomas Bouch's two-mile long crossing over the Firth of Tay were blown down into the waters below, carrying with them a train and all its passengers.

Some of the 245-foot long spans had already been blown down into the Firth during a storm whilst they were being erected, and this should have highlighted the bridge's vulnerability to the elements. Following this tragic disaster, from which there were no survivors, Bouch was made a scapegoat and his bridge was replaced by a more substantial structure designed by W. H. Barlow.

However, the collapse of the Tay Bridge also inspired the replacement of cast-iron bridges all over the country (as well as abroad), whilst the Forth Bridge (which Bouch had been commissioned to design) was handed over to John Fowler and Benjamin Baker. In turn they designed, the world's most impressive-looking bridge with 1,700 foot spans. This was a very 'stiff' bridge, and one that was designed to inspire public confidence, as if to say 'never again would a strong wind or a lack of lateral stability combine to create disaster.'

It has often been said that the design of the Forth Bridge was 'over-cautious', but what is not so widely known is the exacting systems of quality control imposed upon the contractors used in the bridge's construction. This was in response to the fact that the real problem with the Tay Bridge had lain, not so much with its designer, but with the meteorological advice supplied to him (with respect to the potential wind speeds in the Forth of Tay) and the lack of integrity on the part of the contractors (especially the iron-founders) who supplied the materials for the bridge.

Top Right: *The valley of the River Dearne was spanned at Denby Dale by a line of rails carried 112 feet (34.7m) above the valley floor. As can be seen in this picture from around 1870, the original timber trestle was quite a spidery-looking construction; little wonder that local people called for its replacement.*

Bottom Right: *Replaced in 1884, the old timber viaduct was finally dismantled when a new stone-built viaduct came in to use.*

Above: *The speculative nature of railway promotions in the Hudson era left potential investors in fear for their security, so it became common for the companies to build grand buildings so that there was something tangible to show. A good example is the superb Exchange Station Hotel, which opened in Liverpool in 1888.*

The key to railway success was seen by the mid-Victorian era, as having grand station buildings, hotels, warehouses and the like. Investors liked to put their money into property, and the more imposing the station buildings, the more lucrative and stable a proposition appeared to be. The railways therefore spread further and wider, and the local schemes became joined into a national network. Main lines were built up the east coast and the west coast towards Scotland, with progressive cross-country connections being opened along the way.

However, much use of coastal shipping was still being made for connecting railway services; take for example the west coast route, where trains north of Preston went only as far as Fleetwood. From there a connecting steam packet service linked passengers to the Scottish railway network at Ardrossan prior to the full opening of the Caledonian Railway in 1849-50.

Even when the rail link was opened down the West Coast, the partnership of companies that operated it took steps to prevent interlopers from 'stealing their traffic'. For instance, when the North British Railway (NBR) extended their route from Edinburgh to Hawick through to Carlisle in 1862, the WCML partnership refused to move NBR traffic south of the Border City. As a result, the NBR gave their support to the ailing Carlisle & Silloth Bay Dock & Railway Company, and shipped the traffic out to Silloth Docks.

Silloth lays where the Solway Firth enters the Irish Sea, and the Solway had a long maritime association with Ireland, the Isle Of Man and Liverpool, so coastal trans-shipping continued well up to the time (1876) when the Midland Railway arrived in Carlisle with their route from Leeds and Settle, and thus provided a southern rail outlet for NBR traffic.

By the end of the 19th century, the majority of the principle railway schemes had been exhausted, but large parts of the country (mainly rural, less-populated areas) were still clamouring for a rail service. Those towns and villages that were unconnected slipped further and further from prominence, as they became 'backwaters' in the industrialised society the Victorians had made. Ironically, it was in these country areas, devoid of canals and railways that the road network was at its worst. These rural areas still contained unmade roads that were operated by horse-drawn vehicles or a few steam haulage/traction engines, at a time when the internal combustion engine had not yet made its mark.

Even so, the railways looked upon many of these proposed 'rural' schemes with great scepticism, as their construction costs were undoubtedly going to be very expensive, whilst only nominal levels of traffic could be expected in return. The cost of building a branch railway to the standards set by the Railway Inspectorate at the end of the 19th century was quite overwhelming, but that was not to say that a cheaper form of railway or tramway could not be provided.

Below: *Silloth and its docks (on the Cumberland coast) was an unusual product of the railway era when it opened to passenger traffic in 1856. It was meant to replace the facilities at Port Carlisle (the original western terminus of the proposed Tyne - Solway canal), which had become badly silted up by the end of the 1840s. A new 'wet' dock was planned, but it took a considerable time to build into the sand dunes (as shown below). In order to get traffic started, the railway then built a seaside resort where the public came to 'take the waters', but it did so without any parliamentary authority.*

As a result of the need for lines in many rural areas, the Light Railways Act was passed in 1896 (amended 1912), and this allowed railways to be built to lighter specifications and with modified signalling, fencing and the like, but at the same time imposed certain speed and weight restrictions on the operation of a Light Railway. These low cost railways were certainly one answer, but the growing reliability of the internal combustion engine was such that the railways, especially the GWR, began to look at the possibility of operating feeder services linking outlying towns and villages with the nearest railway. Services with road vehicles were soon being operated for passengers and freight, although the railways had no legal powers to do this!

The objective of the Light Railway Act was to open rural or undeveloped areas at minimal cost, and the concept was very successful overseas. Here in Britain the results were far less dramatic, but some notable examples emerged from the 687 applications submitted under the Act between 1897 and 1918. These applications wanted the 'powers' to construct over five thousand route miles of light railway, but in the end less than one thousand were actually built. Road competition became very fierce after World War I, and by the start of World War II only 16 independent light railways were still in operation. The last, the Derwent Valley Light Railway in Yorkshire finally closed in 1988. One Light Railway, the Kent & East Sussex went on to become a preserved railway, whilst several other preservation schemes have sought light railway orders to enable them to re-open closed lines on a more economic operating basis.

Top Left: *When the Newcastle & Carlisle line opened, it severed the route of Lord Carlisle's waggonway to Brampton Town. However, to operate a branch line into the town was a costly proposition, so the NER did not take over the service until 1912 (when it could use a lighter method of operation). It was abandoned during World I, then re-opened and finally closed for good in 1923.*

Centre Left: *The Lynton & Barnstaple may be considered as the most splendid example of a public railway. It carried a two foot gauge line across the wild wastes of Lorna Doone Country for a minimal cost, and where a standard gauge line would have been both impractical (due to the low volume of traffic it would carry) and on account of the high construction costs.*

Bottom Left: *Little known by contrast is another moorland line, the Leadhills & Wanlockhead Light Railway that reached 1,498 foot above sea level, and on it the Caledonian Railway (later LMS) operated mixed trains under a Light Railway Order.*

Above: *In 1893 an expansion of Durham's railway facilities took place, as seen in this celebratory picture of 1446, a North Eastern Railway 2-4-0 (built.1885 and withdrawn 1927).*

INTO THE 20TH CENTURY

By the time the rail network was mostly complete, the companies had increased their engineering and support services to such an extent that, by the end of the 19th century, the railways were (collectively) the biggest owners of engineering workshops in the world. As such they would be seen as a vital resource in the troubled wartime years ahead. By the first decade of the 20th century the railway companies had also concentrated on improving the quality of their services to their passenger customers, their safety record, and above all their comprehensive provision of additional or complimentary services.

From hotels and restaurants, to golf courses and seaside resorts, the railways had built them all. So whether it was freight or passengers, railway services were all encompassing! They owned road vehicles in the tens of thousands, horse-drawn and motorised, carrying 'luggage in advance' or providing a simple onward delivery or collection service that linked in to the railway freight services. They were also the world's biggest owner of ships, docks and canals and during the 1920s and 1930s they helped pioneer internal UK airline services.

However, the biggest single commodity they carried was coal, millions and millions of tons of it – much of which was hand-shovelled out of the railway wagons into waiting carts or lorries. Coal was the food of the industrial revolution and the lifeblood of the railways. The railways loaded the coal with ever-improving ways of mechanical handling, but the same basic four-wheeled ten-foot wheelbase wagon without any form of train braking remained the primary vehicle employed on the nation's transport arteries. Oddly enough, it was the massive volume of coal and the primitive method of working it that would signal its demise. By the 1960s, it would be seen as being so counter-productive and costly to work, that it would provide the excuse for massive cuts in the railway network and the closure of hundreds of stations and goods yards.

Above: *Just as the railways had built ports, docks and jetties, they also began a programme of ship operation. In many cases the railways simply bought out existing shipping lines, but they also developed many others. From 1846 to 1984 the railway-owned ships were operated by up to 60 different lines, and at their height numbered about 1,250 vessels. The most significant were the cross-channel and North Sea ferries, but those used on the services to Ireland and the Channel Islands all contributed to a very profitable sector of railway business. The extension of railway services from mainland Scotland provided a valuable connection with the islands around the coast, with vessels such as the Turbine Steamship (TSS) Duchess of Hamilton being a fine example. Built by the LMS in 1932 it was taken into the nationalised Caledonian Macbrayne fleet in 1948 and finally taken out of service in 1972.*

Even so, it was not all progress; take for example the NBR route to Silloth, and its associated branch line to Port Carlisle that ran on the trackbed of the original canal (opened on 12th March 1823), which was to have been the first leg of the waterway between the Solway Firth and the River Tyne. This canal was drained in 1854 and a railway built along its course, but the branch had become so lightly used by 1857, the railways decided to drop the use of steam locomotives and reverted to horse-drawn operation. The ironic thing is, that once the 'illegally-built' town at Silloth had been created, and the shifting sands of the Solway had caused the docks at Port Carlisle to become silted over, the short 'branch' to the original port was largely superfluous and only local traffic was thereafter carried through a sparsely occupied part of the country.

A series of Dandy Carts were used over the years that followed and these ran between Drumburgh Junction and Port Carlisle until April 1914, when steam trains were re-introduced. A surviving Dandy Car from this line is now to be found fully restored in the National Railway Museum (NRM) at York, although its significance is not widely understood.

Top Right *One of the original 'Dandy' carts seen in the North British Railway's carriage works. Without too much imagination needed, it is easy to see how the 'Dandy' car (and the early British railway carriages) owed their genesis to the old horse-drawn stage coaches. Basically, what we see here, and at museums like the NRM in York, is three 'stagecoaches' joined together and placed on railway running gear.*

Centre Right: *The last Dandy car used at Port Carlisle, and now preserved in the NRM at York, was basically just a fully-glazed, single saloon with benches bolted longitudinally to the outside for third class passengers. The picture postcard proclaims this as the 'only one-horse railway in the world', which was not at all true, but another slogan read; "Port Carlisle possesses a railway perforce - Where the sole locomotive's a common place horse, and in all merry England there's surely none other Train system with so little danger or bother, - So here's to the creature that's useful and handy, Success and renown still attend 'the old Dandy'."*

Bottom Right: *The problem with branch lines like that to Port Carlisle, was the fact that they could not withstand the challenge of the motor lorry or omnibus. During the Depression that followed the Wall Street Crash of October 1929, these lines stood no chance of paying their own way. The stub of the railway from Drumburgh Junction to Port Carlisle, although by then worked with Sentinel steam railcars, was closed by the LNER in June 1932 when the cost of operating the branch outweighed its few receipts.*

Above: *The American Civil War saw the application of railways as machines of war, with things like ambulance trains, armoured trains and prisoner of war trains becoming tools of the military. The use of railways to either get behind enemy lines or to fortify and replenish front-line garrisons, was seen as important. However, long lines of undefended communication were always open to attack by guerrilla forces, so block posts were erected at strategic intervals by the Americans, whilst armoured trains were operated up and down these vital routes. The valuable lessons learned in the American conflict (1861 to 1865) were not overlooked by the British armed forces, as their railways were certainly seen as a means of strengthening the empire. Accordingly, when it came to the Boer War in South Africa (1899 to 1902), things such as ambulance trains, prisoner of war trains and armoured trains were utilised by the British army. Here we see a British armoured train with its protective squad of soldiers who would 'man' the armoured 'cars' at either end of the armour-plated locomotive.*

Another little understood fact about the railways is their military use, although some may recognise that the railways initially structured their hierarchy along the same lines of the army. Others may know that many of the railway surveyors or engineers were often recruited from the mechanical or structural engineering branches of the armed forces. Yet it was their use as a military weapon that is not widely appreciated. The use of railways in times of war had first been seen with stunning results in the American Civil War, where railways were seen as a means of getting troops rapidly to the battle lines.

More importantly, by the strategic use of railways, it was found (as at Atlanta, Georgia), that troops could be taken right around the enemy defensive lines and thus begin their attack on the weakly defended rear flanks. In the late-19th Century, the German general von Schlieffen devised a similar strategy so that the Kaiser's troops could be deployed quickly to the heart of their enemies' capital cities.

Top Right: *The amount of civilian traffic carried by the railways during World War I was quite phenomenal. One example of a new traffic flow is seen here at Gretna on the Glasgow & South Western Railway, where a huge munitions factory was established.*

Bottom Right: *The volume of military traffic was also very high, as can be seen from this view of troops entraining at the Curragh Race Course Station after a session at training camp.*

The British also learned much from the Americans, and in the Boer War they employed block posts to defend the railways, ran armoured trains, used ambulance trains and employed the railways to feed the notorious prisoner of war camps.

An important distinction between the two warring forces in America had demonstrated the way to run railways in times of war; in the South the railways had been run by their army generals, whilst in the North railway managers were given military ranks and operated as liaison officers between the operating departments and the armed forces.

Emulating this practice, ahead of World War I, the British government formed the Railway Executive Committee from railway managers. If war was declared they would still look after the interests of the private railway companies, but at the same time operate in such a way as the work would be coordinated for the national good. The railways in turn would be paid a fixed rate of compensation, which would be based on their pre-war receipts. However, this took no account of all the extra traffic that would be run during this period.

Added to this came the movement of munitions and supplies, and the transfer of coast-wise shipping on to railways due to the high shipping losses, especially on the east coast. Then came leave trains, the extra demand for leisure travel and the high level of imported goods from overseas, and soon the railways were working beyond their capacity.

Above: *A typical scene on the railways either side of the Great War, such as this one of GWR 4-4-0 (3560) at Reading demonstrates just how important the railway was. The engine seen here was originally a broad gauge 0-4-4T until 1891, but was converted to a 'standard gauge' 4-4-0 in 1899.*

Added to this, is the fact that a large percentage of the railway workshops capacity was taken over for the production of war equipment, so the repair and replacement schedules for railway equipment became considerably extended. This was in no way helped by the mass-enlistment of railwaymen and railway workshop workers into the armed forces, as this led to a massive skills shortage. The replacement of seasoned staff by women, young boys and retired railwaymen helped plug the gap, but it was far too little and much too late.

The requisition of railway locomotives and rolling stock to work behind the front lines in Belgium and France may have helped feed the front line troops, but it certainly depleted the railways here at home. Complete branch lines were even ripped up, and then re-laid on the continent. The overall effect of the war was so cataclysmic for the British railway system, that when peace was resumed, the railways were in a completely run-down and almost bankrupt state.

The level of funding agreed before the war proved to be completely inadequate. The railways were thus in need of major overhaul, but neither the companies nor the Government could afford this. The level of railway accidents during the war years and the immediate post-war era was staggering, and with the railways in a run-down state this could only be expected to worsen.

Top Right: *A common feature of the pre-Grouped railway companies was the use of tank engines. However, sizes of engines grew as more powerful locomotives were needed. For instance when the North Eastern Railway introduced the Class 04 0-4-4Ts as their standard passenger tank locomotive, between 1894 and 1901, they proved insufficient for the difficult, but picturesque route between Scarborough and Whitby. Consequently they built ten Class W 4-6-0T locomotives especially for this stretch of line along the Yorkshire Coast. Elsewhere more powerful engines, such as this A7 class 4-6-2T (Pacific) were built for heavy mineral traffic.*

Centre Right: *The Atlantic (4-4-2) was a popular wheel arrangement for tank engines with the Great Central Railway (GCR), North British Railway (NBR), and Great Northern Railway (GNR) for suburban passenger services.*

Bottom Right: *At the 'heavy' end of the scale, the London & North Western Railway produced this 0-8-2T for freight duties. Like the NER engine above, it has been left painted in grey (for photographic purposes) but fully lined-out: as shiny black would have led to unwanted reflections.*

The railways were not immediately released from State control, and the Railway Executive Committee remained in charge until 1921. However, it was clear that things could not go back to as they were before August 1914. The financial position of many companies was one reason for the need to change, but there was a general agreement that the benefits of unified operation should be carried on in peacetime as well. The second, and probably most significant part of the 1921 Railways Act was that it introduced a rationalised system of charging. The establishment of a Railway Rates Tribunal, in turn provided for a rate of charges that would realise annual net revenues that were (supposedly) at least equivalent to those received in 1913.

However, several commentators, including Winston Churchill, saw nationalisation of this vital infrastructure as being the only solution. Nevertheless, The Railways Act of 1921 led to the formation of four large groups, which would absorb the 120 smaller companies. These groups would be The Great Western, The London, Midland & Scottish, The London & North Eastern and the Southern, although it would have made more logical and geographic sense to create six groups. Parts of the railway were reorganised from January 1922 onwards, when some companies, notably the GWR with several smaller railways, and the London & North Western with the Lancashire & Yorkshire railways, set the merger ball rolling.

THE RAILWAY GROUPING OF 1923

The four new companies established under the Grouping were the Great Western Railway (GWR), the London Midland & Scottish Railway (LMS), London & North Eastern Railway (LNER) and the Southern Railway (SR). These companies then divided Britain almost geographically! The GWR took over the railways in the south and south west, as well as south and central Wales, whilst the LNER had the railways that operated in the eastern half of England and Scotland. Meanwhile the LMS had the western side of Britain, including England, Scotland and North Wales, whilst the Southern, as its name implies, covered the south and south-east.

There were a number of common meeting places, such as London, Bristol, Birmingham and so on, as well as some long lines that penetrated right into the territory of a rival group. For example the SR had its 'long withered arm', which penetrated well inside GWR territory, reaching Exeter, from where lines radiated to Cornwall and North Devon. The GWR had its route up into LMS territory with a line through the Welsh Marches to Birkenhead and the Mersey ports. The LMS reached down to the south coast, and the LNER had control of the cross-country route along the course of the proposed Newcastle to Carlisle canal, and the west coast port of Silloth. A study of a map showing the Grouped Railways will clearly reveal the extent of the territory these companies occupied.

Left: *Each of the Big Four railway companies had their 'Giants of Steam', with the GWR's King Class 4-6-0s being amongst the most striking. Here we see 4081* Warwick Castle *on a special working to Pinewood Film Studios.*

Top Right: *Local branch line trains were an important feeder for the main lines, and here we see a Hughes Railmotor at West Vale. It has obviously been given an additional carriage for use on the normally lightly-used Stainland branch.*

Bottom Right: *On the Southern Railway, local services were very well patronised, and to meet the demand for travel, electrical multiple units were introduced.*

From the outset of the Grouping, it was clear that in some areas a rationalisation of services needed to take place. The legacy left behind by the Victorian desire for competition meant that the railways often had duplicated facilities in many towns. Take for example Dewsbury, where all but one of the town's stations and goods yards came under the control of the LMS (the other became part of the LNER). This allowed the Market Place passenger station (ex-L&YR) to close in December 1930, but real rationalisation of facilities in the town did not take place until the 1950s and after nationalisation.

Rationalisation could have taken place in my town of residence, Appleby-in-Westmorland as two stations were located about 400 yards from one another. The Midland station was on the Settle-Carlisle route, whilst the NER station was on the Darlington-Penrith line. These two could have been brought together by re-opening a redundant connection at the east end of the stations, but no such work was ever implemented. Elsewhere, it was often geographically impossible to combine routes even in the same town, although the City of Bradford was always a prime candidate for a link of a few hundred yards to connect its two main stations Exchange and Forster Square.

Top Left: *In many areas, no economies of operation could be achieved after the Grouping, so cuts were made in the kind of train provision being offered. Here we see an ex-Southern Railway 2-4-T (3488) at Axminster, with a one-coach train in June 1949.* W. P. Mileham

Bottom Left: *In contrast some lines were worked up to and beyond their capacity, as for example the route through the Pennines at Woodhead. Sir Nigel Gresley therefore planned to electrify the line and create a new tunnel below the mountains parallel to the point where the ex-Great Central 4-6-0 (LNER Class B7/2) is seen at Dunford Bridge.* the late David Ibbotson

An example of rationalisation that springs to mind are the stations in the Spen Valley, which all came under LMS control, but as the destinations from these places were either Leeds or Bradford, it was impossible to achieve any degree of centralisation. Ironically, had Hudson been able to complete his grand plan for a single company back in the 1840s and 1850s, rationalisation would not have been so vitally needed 70 years later. So, in essence, the amount of route mileage abandoned in the Grouped period was relatively small.

The big disadvantage for the 'Big Four' companies was not however their large and disparate networks, but the second part of the 1921 Railway Act, which left them wide open to competition from other forms of transport. The structure contained many antiquated charging methods, and forced the railways to publish their rates. This enabled the rapidly growing road transport industry (both goods and passenger operators) to look at ways of under-cutting the Big Four on short or middle-distance routes. As the railways could not offer the same flexibility as road transport, the losses were significant in a period when traditional heavy industries were in sharp decline, especially during the General Strike of 1926 or the Depression that followed the Wall Street Crash of 1929.

Yet despite these factors, and the generally atrocious state of the economy, it was not all doom and gloom for the Big Four. By the 1930s notable improvements had been made with main line trains, with record-breaking services being introduced on both the East Coast and the West Coast main lines. A product of that era was *Mallard*'s record-breaking run for the LNER on 3rd July 1938.

Both the GWR and the Southern improved their express trains, but the latter should be applauded more for the introduction of third-rail electrified trains on both long-distance and suburban routes. Yet away from the main line you could still be forgiven for thinking that many secondary railways were little changed from Edwardian days!

As the 1930s progressed, more state aid came into the railways, but this only funded those works that would be of strategic or operational value in the event of a second war with Germany. When that war broke out in 1939, the story was much the same as it had been in 1914-18, but this time the railways also had to contend with the aerial attacks of the Luftwaffe. Fortunately, this form of attack was not pressed home as hard as it might have been; for had the crippling effect of the U-boat war been combined with the devastation of the in-land transport network, the country could have easily been brought to its knees.

Top Right: *An early priority for the 'Big Four' once World War II was declared, was the evacuation of children from the major cities. Here we see an LMS train getting ready to move children from Liverpool's Edge Hill station to Gresford in North Wales.*

Bottom Right: *Getting people away from the bombing was one aspect of railway work, cleaning up after the attacks was another. Here a GWR 0-6-0PT (3727) rumbles into the western end of London carrying hundreds of planks of timber to assist in boarding-up bomb damaged properties.*

THE FORMATION OF BRITISH RAILWAYS

During World War II the railways were asked to work as they had done before, and they were again compensated in the same way, so there is little surprise that the end results were almost identical. Overworked, under-staffed and worn out are the three terms that best describe the railways of 1946 – oh yes, and they were virtually bankrupt again! The political answer this time was the full nationalisation of all transport, including nearly all road haulage companies, railway undertakings, canals, airports and docks.

The Nationalisation of British railways was of course a part of the post-war Labour government's view of a socialist utopia, along with nationalised service in coal mining, steel-making and health. The railway companies had another idea, which given what has since happened with our railway system, should have been entirely feasible back in 1946-7.

The railways had put forward a view that, if the state took control of the track and the infrastructure, much as they did with the road network, then the railway companies could quite easily run improved train services thereon. Nobody listened, and full-blown nationalisation ensured.

Left: *At an early stage British Railways decided that it would need a standard locomotive fleet. To seek out the best features from the various main line express locomotives that they had inherited, BR undertook a series of exchanges. Here we see ex-Southern West Country Class 4-6-2* Bude, *being operated with an LMS tender and the LNER (formerly NER) dynamometer car.* British Railways

Top Right: *When the 'Grouped' company locomotives were vested into British Railways, they were all carrying the names of their former owners. A programme to re-paint the rolling stock was implemented, usually when it went in for overhaul, but examples of the former names could be seen on working locomotives well into the 1950s. Others were given the new 'British Railways' straight lettering, as seen on this former GWR 0-6-0PT (3726).*

Centre Right: *Sandbridge Road near St. Albans (locally known as 'Dead Womans Hill Bridge') forms the backdrop for the 7.15am Manchester Central to London St. Pancras express on 3rd July 1948. The locomotive, still wearing its LMS identity (10000) is one of their two pioneering diesel-electric locomotives. This design would give the newly nationalised railway the confidence to introduce its own fleet of Type 4 diesel-electric engines in 1959.* E. D. Bruton

Bottom Right: *Given the plan to undertake both electric overhead traction and diesel haulage, it seams strange that BR concentrated so heavily on its fleet of 999 'standard class' steam locomotives. These engines were built within a range of different specifications, the largest being the superb 2-10-0 9Fs, which many people say were scrapped far too early. However, the question really should be, were not the Standards built too late? Perhaps it would have been better for British Railways to continue building engines to the designs of the former companies. A good example of these is seen here with 6257,* City of Salford, *which was completed at Crewe Works in June 1948 but outshopped wearing its original LMS number.* British Railways

Nationalisation had been the cornerstone of the Labour party since its early days at the end of the 19th century, and this ideology was confirmed at their Annual Conference of 1908. Yet even this was not a new idea, for as early as 1836 James Morrison had tried to get Parliament to obtain powers to 'revise railway tolls'. In 1838, the Duke of Wellington, convinced that railways had a vital role to play in both the defence and economic prosperity of the country, tried to persuade Prime Minister Melbourne to guard against the 'monopoly and mismanagement' of the railway companies

Top Left: *The year 1952 marked a time of change for the nationalised railways, especially after the Conservatives were re-elected into Government on an anti-nationalisation platform. The year also marked the Coronation of Queen Elizabeth and the 'new Elizabethan era'. Here Coventry Station is specially decorated for the celebrations.* British Railways

Centre Left: *To meet the demands of the new British Railways, a number of 'standard' locomotive designs were conceived, using the best of the technology found in the Grouped stock. These Standard Class engines created a 999-strong fleet, made up of 12 different types, plus two classes of ex-War Department engines numbering 758. Here we see a Standard Class Type 2 Mogul, 2-6-0 78008, part of a 65-strong class.*

Bottom Left: *Closure by stealth began apace in the early 1950s, but resistance to these closures was captured in the Ealing Comedy,* The Titfield Thunderbolt, *which was filmed on the Camerton to Limpley Stoke line in 1952. That epic of the British cinema was in turn inspired by the rescue of the narrow-gauge Talyllyn Railway, a former slate line, by a group of volunteers lead by railway author Tom Rolt.* Movie Scene Pictures

In 1868 a Royal Commission was appointed to re-investigate the issue of nationalisation, but it was concluded that nothing should be done about the matter. Finally, the Transport Act of 1947 vested the Big Four railways into the new British Railways, taking with them 20,023 steam locomotives, and a few diesel and electric locomotives. They also inherited 4,184 electrical multiple unit vehicles (mostly from the Southern), 36,033 items of passenger stock and no less than 1,223,634 freight vehicles.

The Railway Executive had to maintain a staggering total of 19,639 route miles, although some rationalisation was possible with the closure of duplicated lines and stations. Eight lines went in 1948, 19 in 1949, 43 in 1950, 100 in 1951 and 66 in 1952; a total of 236 railways in five years. After nationalisation the railways were split into five regions, each of which was based on the Big Four 'grouped' companies' operating areas, although the new Scottish Region was carved out of the LMS and the LNER. A sixth region would be split away from the Eastern Region in 1956, and with the resulting North Eastern Region the six new 'regions' looked to provide a better management structure for the railways. Yet this nationalised system did not sit well with the right-wing Conservative Party, and no sooner had the brave experiment begun in January 1948, than the opposition put de-nationalisation into their manifesto.

On achieving power at the General Election in 1950, the Conservatives systematically began their demolition of the British Transport Commission, attacking first the road haulage operations of the British Road Services. British Railways was then to come on their target list, as the power of the unions presented what the government perceived as 'a major threat to national stability'. This was demonstrated in 1956 when a serious railway strike damaged the Government's standing to such an extent, that it threatened to bring it down. The joining of railway, steel and coal unions as part of a 'Triple Alliance' (one out – all out) led to a decision to smash the monopoly of these nationalised industries. It took time to fully achieve this goal, and the coal miners were not finally beaten until Mrs. Thatcher destroyed the nation's coal mining communities in the 1980s and 1990s, but steel and rail had crumbled well before.

The next issue to play a part in the demise of the railways also goes back to 1950. When elected, the new government were horrified to find the amount of finance that the Labour party had proposed spending on the railways, even though the British Railways Modernisation Plan was (in reality) just the compensation that the railways were due as a result of their efforts in World War II. It is not surprising that, during the next few years, the issue of funding was repeatedly deferred. In 1958, the long-awaited 'Modernisation' money was put in place, but only on the condition that the railways achieve overall profitability within five years. In essence, 41 years of neglect had to be repaired in five. Everyone could see that this was impossible, but to gain their vitally needed funding, the railway management agreed to these onerous terms. Management well understood that the system inherited under nationalisation was much too large, even though 4,000 miles of line had been closed to passengers between the Grouping of 1923 and 1959.

Top Right: *In addition to the closure of branch lines, a new era of main line dieselisation arrived. Here one of the English Electric Type 4s (D247), heads towards Standedge in 1960.*

Centre Right: *With the advent of diesel, hundreds of steam locomotives (such as these ex-LMS 2Ps at engine shed 67B, Hurlford also in 1960) were laid-up pending a return to work that would rarely materialise.* Oliver Carter

Bottom Right: *Even rural branches lost steam working, and the final train on the Wisbech & Upwell Tramway was worked by D2201 on 20th May 1966. The sole consignment of freight on this train were boxes of flowers carried in the guard's van.* L. Sandler

Top Left: *The big challenge for passenger travel, especially on long distance routes, came as private car ownership increased. This was especially seen after the arrival of the new motorways, the first of which was the Preston by-pass (1959). Next came the M1, which paralleled the route of the first railway of consequence, the London & Birmingham. It is seen (just before its opening) with the newest cars from Vauxhall Motors near the junction with the A6 to Birmingham.*

Bottom Left: *Would the British Transport Commission have closed the Holmfirth line, seen here with 2-6-2T 42158 in 1958, had it not had a half share in the buses running from Huddersfield to Holmfirth?*

Many more un-remunerative or duplicated lines and services remained, but the procedure for closure was notoriously slow. So no real rationalisation took place, and closure during this period seems to have been both sporadic and haphazard. Simultaneously with the railways running deeper and deeper into debt, they were confronted with formidable new competitors. These included massive competition from the road transport interests, which had now achieved a huge lobbying power following the de-nationalisation of British Road Services.

However, the railway closures of that period do not always add up, and a good example of BR's 'spurious accounting' is found with the short (1.5 mile long) branch line to Holmfirth in Yorkshire. In June 1959 British Railways announced their proposals to withdraw passenger services on the branch as it was losing £10,000pa. Yet the local town council stated that BR had submitted 'False Facts' about the branch, as parcels traffic was extremely lucrative, but the £6,000 annual revenue from this was not shown anywhere in the lines's accounts". Adding "the information in the [closure] memorandum is totally misleading, and certainly the facts are false."

Above: *An immediate target for Dr. Beeching was the antiquated local freight services that were operated all over Britain, a classic example of which is seen behind 0298 Class 2-4-0WT 30585 near Penhargard on the Wadebridge - Wenford Bridge line in September 1958.* S. C. Nash

DOCTOR BEECHING'S AXE

The Holmfirth branch that we mentioned in the previous chapter was just one example of pre-Beeching cuts, and not particularly unique either. The same issues of questionable accounting could be repeated hundreds of times over, so to justify the mass closures that were secretly planned, the railways were subjected to a 1959 report by Dr. Richard Beeching (1913-1985) entitled *The Re-shaping of British Railways*. In 1961 the Conservative government appointed Beeching as the Chairman of British Railways with a brief to cut the spiralling losses. His report was implemented from 1963 onwards, with a mass of closures occurring in 1964-5, whilst the surviving traffic tended to be concentrated into fast express services or block goods trains working to or from major marshalling yards.

Beeching believed that the railway system should be run like a business and not as a public service. He also took the view that, if parts of the railway system that didn't pay their way (like most rural branch lines) were closed, then the remaining core of the system could be restored to profitability. He made a study of traffic on all the railway lines in the country and concluded that 80% of the traffic was carried on just 20% of the network, with much of the rest of the system carrying very little traffic indeed and was thus claimed to be 'operating at a loss'.

Above: *Despite the fact that Britain's last steam locomotive 9F Class 2-10-0* Evening Star *was only built in 1961 (and had a 50-year projected lifespan), it was decreed that all steam haulage would be progressively removed and eliminated completely by the middle of 1968. Here we show another member of the 9F Class, 92066, as it works one of the heavy ore trains that ran from Tyne Dock to the Consett steel works.*

At the time the report was called the 'Beeching Bombshell' or the 'Beeching Axe' by the press and was hugely controversial, sparking an outcry from those communities that would lose their rail services. The report proposed that 6,000 miles of Britain's then 18,000 miles of railway system be closed (mostly rural branch and cross country lines) and that many other rail lines should lose their passenger services and be kept open for freight only. In addition, many lesser-used stations would close on those lines that were to be kept open. The report (surprise, surprise) was quickly accepted by the government.

There was also a significant part of the Beeching Plan, which proposed that British Railways electrify some major main lines and adopt containerised freight traffic instead of the outdated and uneconomic wagon-load traffic. But whilst the politicians jumped at the cost-saving parts of the plan, they were less enthusiastic about the parts that cost money, although some of them were adopted, for example the electrification of the West Coast Mainline.

Huge areas of Britain saw rural lines being closed or swept free of steam; notable was East Anglia, where the 'modernisation programme' was implemented regardless of the costs in social hardship or rural deprivation. Not all of the railway lines listed for closure were closed! A few were kept open for a variety of reasons, some of which were political. For example the railway lines through the Scottish Highlands, although uneconomic, were kept open due in part to pressure from the powerful Highland lobby. Some other lines may have been kept open because they passed through marginal constituencies.

Top Right: *To obtain the closure of a line or withdrawal of services prior to Beeching, was a difficult affair for BR. Usually great local opposition was raised, and Transport Users Consultative Committee enquiries such as this held during the withdrawal of passenger trains on the Penistone to Barnsley line in 1959 were well attended. Even so, most of BR's proposals were 'rubber-stamped' and the Barnsley line closed to passengers in June 1959. However, the closure was reversed in 1983 when Huddersfield - Penistone - Sheffield trains were re-routed via Barnsley.*

Centre Right: *A picture of a TUCC hearing at Huddersfield, where the closure of the Huddersfield - Penistone line was being considered. The hearing rejected the closure proposals, which is ironic given that Beeching wished to close the Huddersfield line, whilst at the same time he held up the Sheffield - Penistone - Manchester line as a shining example of a modern railway. This 1500v DC electrified railway, fully-modernised in the early 1950s lost its passenger services at the end of 1969 and its freight trains 12 years later.*

Bottom Right: *After the 1962 Transport Act, the TUCCs were limited only to advising the Minister of the hardship that closure would cause. This took no account of the merits of a closure proposal, especially those that were not justified on economic grounds and many 'last trains' were run, like this one to Middleton-in-Teesdale on 2nd November 1964. Maurice S. Burns*

When the railways were nationalised, the Act had made provision for the protection for users of what was to become a monopoly. Accordingly, under Section Six of the 1947 Act, they formed a Central Transport Consultative Committee, with regional committees below it. Their remit was to consider closure proposals and make recommendations with regard to any matter, including rates and charges, affecting services that were operated by the British Transport Commission.

The Minister of State for Transport assured the public that these Committees had not been set up to 'rubber-stamp' issues like closure proposals, but in practice hindsight shows there to have been little difference in the views of the consultative committees and the aims of the British Railways Executive. Even when a committee recommended retention of services, as in the case of Westerham Branch (Kent) in 1961, the Minister could overturn the recommendations and close the line anyway. The review and consultation process, even though it was likely to go in favour of the closure process was believed by Beeching to be too long-winded and time consuming.

Top Left: *As seen in the previous picture of Middleton-in-Teesdale, diesel multiple units had become widely used by the early 1960s. Yet, their use on long cross-country trips, such as these three Derby units at Pinwherry in July 1962 could hardly have been comfortable for travellers on the Glasgow - Stranraer Boat Train.*

Bottom Left: *By way of contrast, the specially constructed cross-country DMUs, like this Trans-Pennine set at Goole in 1961 were in fact the height of luxury.*

As a result of the delays these 'hearings' could cause, one of the recommendations in the 1962 Transport Act sought to diminish the power of the TUCCs. Despite this, several lines approved for closure were kept open because the local roads weren't capable of absorbing the traffic that would be transferred from the railway if it closed. A classic example of how the process brought a temporary reprieve to a number of lines is seen with the Alston branch line. Located deep in the heart of the North Pennines, England's highest market town was served by a very rural branch line. During the 19th century, the town was the centre of one of the major lead mining districts and as early as June 1824, James Thompson had prepared estimates for the extension of Lord Carlisle's waggonway from Hallbankgate to Midgeholme, with a view to later extending to Alston.

Following the opening first section of the Newcastle & Carlisle Railway between 1835 and 1836, the new stations in the Tyne Valley provided greatly improved railheads for Alston. After this line was doubled in 1844, the company turned their attention to the South Tyne Valley in November 1845. Plans were prepared by their engineer (John Bourne) for a branch line to run from Haltwhistle to Nenthead (17 miles), via Alston. However, at precisely the same time another company deposited plans that proposed linking Alston directly to the Newcastle & Carlisle and Stockton & Darlington railways.

This would have seen a 38-mile extension of the S&DR through Alston to join the Newcastle & Carlisle Railway at Milton. The Newcastle & Carlisle scheme was eventually adopted, but this idea was cut back to terminate at Alston when it finally 'opened to all traffic' on 17th November 1852.

In addition to the steep gradients, the earthworks were heavy and no less than nine stone viaducts were constructed to carry the rails over the River South Tyne and its tributaries. Sufficient land was taken for double track, but this was never required and the line remained single to the end. Despite further surveys for a line from Alston to Weardale or Teesdale, the Alston branch remained in its original form to the end.

Above: *Alston engine shed and goods shed were demolished, but a single track line remained between the pile of rubble and the platform.*

The branch served the South Tyne Valley for 124 years and it was not until May 1976 that an adequate road was completed into the upper reaches of the valley. A replacement bus route heralded the closure of the Alston branch, with a promise that this would be run in perpetuity. However, early in 2005 it was announced that this service would be finally discontinued as the subsidies were being withdrawn, and this is a story so typical of these 'bus replacement services'.

Above: *From 1961 around 16,000 steam locomotives, 1,000 of which were under 12 years old, were ear-marked for scrapping as British Railways began to 'modernise' its locomotive fleet. The level of carnage is illustrated by this view of the John Cashmore Yard at Great Bridge in the West Midlands.*

The Railways Beeching Closed

* 1961   150 miles closed
* 1962   780 miles closed
* 1963   324 miles closed
* 1964   1,058 miles closed
* 1965   600 miles closed
* 1966   750 miles closed
* 1967   300 miles closed
* 1968   400 miles closed
* 1969   250 miles closed
* 1970   275 miles closed
* 1971   23 miles closed
* 1972   50 miles closed
* 1973   35 miles closed
* 1974   0 miles closed

In addition to the Beeching line closures, 2,128 stations were closed on lines that remained open. In 1964 a new Labour government was elected with Prime Minister Harold Wilson, who had come to power (partly) on an election campaign in which Labour promised to halt the rail closures if elected. But once elected they quickly backtracked on this promise and the closures continued until the end of the decade, However in 1965 Mrs. Barbara Castle was appointed Transport Minister, and she set about looking at the country's transport problems as a whole. Mrs Castle decided that at least 11,000 route miles of 'basic railway' would be needed for the future, and that the system should be stabilised at around this size. Despite the mass closures, a fair number of rural railway lines remain in existence on the British railway system today, although far fewer than there were before Beeching.

Towards the end of the 1960s it was becoming increasingly clear that the rail closures were not producing the promised savings that Beeching had foretold. What is more they were failing to bring the rail system out of deficit, and were unlikely ever to do so. Meanwhile, the rapid policy of dieselisation and the corresponding withdrawal of steam saw around 16,000 steam locomotives being withdrawn and prematurely sent to the scrapyard.

Meanwhile, Mrs. Castle stipulated that those services, that could not pay their way but had a valuable social role should be subsidised. However by the time the legislation allowing this was introduced in 1968, many of the services and lines that would have qualified for subsidies had already been closed or removed, so the impact of her proposal was not that significant and the reprieved lines or services were few in number.

Yet a number of branch and secondary lines were saved by this legislation, a prime example being the Huddersfield to Penistone route from which the Holmfirth branch had diverged. The closures failed in their central purpose of restoring the railways to profitability, with the promised savings failing to materialise. This was mainly because the branch lines acted as feeders to the main lines, and this feeder traffic was lost when the branches closed; in turn meaning less traffic for the main lines and a corresponding drop in their finances as well!

Below: *As mentioned, one of the lines that Barbara Castle reprieved, and which is still operating today, is the route from Huddersfield to Penistone. On this route only the station at Berry Brow was closed, despite having a very high level of peak-hour usage. It is seen here on the last day of services on 4th July 1966.*

THE YEARS OF NEGLECT

The closures were brought to a halt in the early 1970s when it became apparent that they weren't achieving anything useful, and that the benefit of the small amount of money saved by closing railways was outweighed by the pollution and congestion caused by the increasing reliance on cars that then followed. After the early 1970s, railways went not with a bang, but with a whimper, as the last major railway closure to occur was the former North British Railway's 80-mile long main line between Carlisle and Edinburgh.

Better known as the Waverly Route, it closed in 1969, but was this really ripe for closure? The answer can be given in the fact that plans are now being promoted through the Scottish Parliament to re-open this line, in order to try and reduce the huge number of road-based commuter journeys being made from the border towns into Edinburgh each day.

Above: *Although some of the Beeching closures were justifiable, with hindsight many of his cuts seem foolish or short-sighted, and whilst others are now being bitterly regretted. Lines like the old North British 'Waverley' route from Carlisle to Edinburgh served a vital role in the Borders, and today there is strong local pressure for it to be re-opened. The route closed in 1969, but as seen with this pick-up goods behind J37 Class 64561 at Galashiels in July 1961, local freight had already substantially contracted.* J. C. Baker

In the early-1980s under the government of Margaret Thatcher, the spectre of more Beeching-style cuts was raised again for a short while. In 1983 a civil servant called David Serpell, who had worked with Dr Beeching, made the Serpell Report, which called for more rail closures. It was met with fierce resistance from many quarters, and the report was quickly abandoned. Most commentators now agree that both the Beeching and Serpell plans went too far.

Top Right: *Darlington was the birthplace of the public steam railway, but by the time this picture was taken on 20th August 1964, dieselisation had well and truly taken hold. Diesel multiple units await departures to Crook and Middleton in Teesdale, and an Anglo-Scottish express runs through behind an English Electric locomotive.*

Bottom Right: *Whilst most of BR contented itself with diesel-electric traction as a replacement for steam, the Western Region took on diesel-hydraulic technology. Here a very grimy Warship Class, D832 Onslaught, leaves Exeter St. David's in July 1970.* N. E. Preedy

Supporters of the Beeching cuts believe that they were a necessary emergency response to save the railway network from financial disaster, and that if they hadn't taken place, a far bigger programme of cuts would have been necessary later on. Yet, one of the major criticisms made of the Beeching report was that it failed to take into account future trends like population growth and greater demand for travel. For instance the population of many of the towns that had their railways closed in the 1960s have grown significantly since, leaving these towns urgently in need of rail or light rail links. Ludicrously, many stations were closed in parts of the country where it was obvious a demand for rail transport was emerging.

Take for example Washington, County Durham, where the passenger station closed in 1963, having opened as early as 1835. Goods trains ended in 1964, even though a line still runs through the town today. Had this been a small country halt, one could have expected this kind of rationalisation, but during the early 1960s Washington was being developed into one of Britain's new towns, where huge residential estates and industrial buildings were erected in a very short period of time. These towns were given modern roadway systems and even links to motorways, but no direct rail services (Milton Keynes would be a very specific exemption however).

Top Left: *A tractor train on the Meltham branch, which was closed in 1965. By 1970 the volume of traffic on offer was over 500 tractors per week, but British Rail rejected the proposals to either re-open the line or allow the trackbed to be used as a road for delivering the tractors down to the junction station at Lockwood.*

Bottom Left: *By way of contrast some lines were ripe for closure, including the pioneering Stanhope & Tyne Railroad seen here in 1968 at Waskerley. It had lost passenger trains as early as July 1859, and the final goods service (down to a couple of wagons per week) went in April 1968.*

Beeching also made some blatantly unjustifiable cuts in freight traffic too, and in this we might take a look at the example of the next geographic branch line to Holmfirth, the 3.5-mile long line to Meltham. It had lost its passenger trains in May 1949, and this can be considered quite logical given that better bus services existed in the area. However, the line was intensely used for freight, and it carried coal, sand, sandstone, textiles and engineering components, but most of all tractors – a minimum of 300 of them every week.

This required at least ten trains (Monday to Friday), plus one on a Saturday morning to take out all the agricultural equipment made at the Meltham tractor factories. This traffic alone provided the railway with an income three times its operating costs, yet it was closed in 1965 without any consideration because it was claimed to be unprofitable.

When David Browns asked about the possibility for reopening the branch, they met with a blank refusal. As did the idea of turning the track bed into a delivery route leading to a loading facility at Lockwood station (near the former junction for the branch), which was situated conveniently alongside the David Brown Gear Works factory. Consequently, in 1971, I was responsible for ordering ten new road vehicle transporters to cope with the increasing output from the tractor plant.

Some closures also showed the complete idiosyncrasy of BR's mathematics and accounting, take for example the railway running from the West Coast Main Line at Penrith to the Lake District town of Keswick. This route was built as a mineral line between 1862 and 1864 to link Workington in the west to Co.Durham in the east, connecting (via Penrith) to the railway route over the Pennines at Stainmore and on to the Darlington area. Its builder was Thomas Bouch, the well-known civil engineer who we met in connection with the Tay Bridge.

The iron, coke and coal traffic that gave the impetus to this railway line declined between the two world wars, but passenger demand was very high as it passed through the beautiful countryside of Cumberland and Westmorland, including the Lake District National Park after it was designated in 1949. Because passenger traffic alone made it a very seasonal line, the process of closure started in the 1950s.

Above: *Was it a co-incidence that the Keswick line closed in March 1973 before the tourist season started again, and before the new electrified West Coast Main Line services showed that the branch still had a vital role to play? Fortunately much of the infrastructure remains three decades later, including several of Bouch's superb 'bow-string' bridges. Plans come and go for its re-opening as a means of providing an environmentally friendly way of visiting this beautiful part of England.*

At the time the BR accountants estimated that it was losing £50,000 per year and as a result said they intended to close the whole line from Penrith to Workington. Before such a step was taken however, BR looked at possible measures of making economies on the line and as one of the consequences of this, they decided that a change from steam-hauled trains to railcar operation would be worth trying.

Top Left: *On 3rd January 1955, Derby Lightweight diesel multiple-units were introduced on the Keswick passenger services, and this in turn immediately turned the passenger train losses into profits. This saw Ivatt's 2-6-0 tender engines, like 46449 at Penrith, becoming redundant on the route.* H. C. Casserley

Bottom Left: *How much would the Keswick line have benefited with the coming of faster services along the WCML. In the 1980s a dream of high-speed (145mph) travel came with the Advance Passenger Train, seen here passing through Tebay. This train offered the next step in railway technology, and a move on from the High Speed Trains that had been introduced to run 125mph services on the GWR and ECML routes in the late-1970s. After extensive trials, during which a record speed of over 160 mph was achieved on 20th December 1979, the first regular 125mph APT service started between Glasgow and Euston in 1981 with a 255-minute timing. It was envisaged that by the mid-1980s, a fleet of APTs would serve the electrified main line services to the North West and West Midlands. Sadly, after some initial teething problems, the APT was considered to be a 'white elephant' and (arguably on political dictate) was completely and utterly dropped in the mid-1980s.*

The big problem in any closure proposal was that BR's accounts and statistics were so complex, segmented and difficult to follow that the only people who could make any sense of the arguments for closure were those who were promoting them. Now, whilst statistics can be used to provide very useful information, they can also be swapped around to provide misleading facts (as in the case of the Holmfirth branch). The way BR calculated how much a line was making or losing quite often followed this principle, and receipts might be attributed to another station. In the case of the Keswick line, many of its receipts were attributed to Penrith, which was part of the already profitable West Coast route.

In its case British Railways announced that, despite the economies in working the Penrith – Workington section, the line was still losing money. Thus Beeching recommended that the line should be swept away. On 1st July 1964, all goods services were withdrawn, whilst one year later BR announced that it intended to close the whole line to passenger services in April 1966. This sparked off a storm of protest from local people who were keen to keep the line open. However, at the same time the Ministry of Transport also had its eye on the trackbed for an improvement scheme for the main A66 road west of Keswick.

The viable line from Penrith to Keswick was a different matter, but when a review came up at the end of the 1960s BR decided to calculate its usage at a highly questionable time. It did its calculation of the usage of services during the dead of winter, when few tourists were around and at a time when the mainline railway through Penrith was suffering many delays or closures due to its conversion to overhead electric operation. Accordingly, the figures that were presented to the Transport Minister in support of closure seemed favourable towards BR's proposals and closure ensued in March 1972.

Top Right: *The closures of the Beeching era saw the trackbeds of many closed railways being built over or otherwise severed, thus making them difficult to re-open. Yet, some lines did remain open for mineral or freight traffic, including the old North Eastern Railway branch between Bishop Auckland and Eastgate in Weardale. Local people, supported by the area's councils, managed to see the re-opening of the line to Stanhope and the re-introduction of summer Sunday trains as part of the Dales Rail service. Here, we see the re-opening of Witton Park (Etherley) Station on 25th August 1991.*

Bottom Right: *Berry Brow, which closed in 1966 (see page 55) was re-located and re-opened to passenger trains on 9th October 1989.*

Top Left: *The wonderful link that the railways offered with other forms of transport is captured in this late-1930s view across Windermere to Lakeside Station, where LMS trains connected with the steamers that operated to Bowness-on-Windermere and Ambleside. However, the benefit of this line was not appreciated by Beeching, and he closed it to passengers in 1965.*

Bottom Left: *Today the truncated section of the Lakeside branch runs for 3.5 miles from Haverthwaite, to the terminus at Lakeside via Newby Bridge. Not only does it provide an environmentally friendly way of getting visitors directly into the heart of the Lake District National Park, but it offers a very scenic and relaxed first and last leg to any journey. Here an ex-LMS Fairburn 2-6-4T, 42073, approaches the terminus in October 2004.*

As for those lines that stayed open down to this day, like nearly every other railway system in the world, they still run at a deficit. Some may say that to support such loss-making lines and services is a costly drain on our national resources; yet the question remains, 'is it not better to support environmentally-friendly transport schemes, than to continue to pile more and more private car traffic on to our roads, especially in environmentally-sensitive areas like the Lake District?'

At the south end of this National Park, another former 'rural branch', the Lakeside & Haverthwaite operates as a preserved 'steam' railway. Originally this branch line of the Furness Railway opened in 1905 to carry passengers and freight from Lakeside to Ulverston and Barrow, or south to Lancashire.

The line was closed in 1965, although the terminus station at Lakeside was retained by British Railways as their steamships plied across Lake Windermere from Bowness Bay. Although the BR steamers were no longer rail-connected after 1965, the Windermere branch of the Lancaster & Carlisle Railway (part of the WCML) still remains open today.

PRIVATISATION - A NEW FUTURE?

A modest number of railway closures have been reversed in recent years, as quite a number of closed stations have re-opened and passenger services restored on lines where they had been removed. Several lines, like the Lakeside & Haverthwaite, have reopened as heritage railways, although some (like the Alston branch) have just seen narrow gauge tourist lines being built on the former standard gauge trackbed. Yet despite these success stories on the branch lines, worse was to come for the main lines and in the mid-1990s Railway Privatisation was the brainchild of the Conservative Government under Prime Minister John Major. The Railways Act of 1994 was highly controversial and took the best part of a year to go through both Houses before gaining Royal Assent.

Above: *The Class 90 locomotives were built at BREL Crewe, and were originally designed to be used on both high speed passenger, and slower speed freight trains on the WCML.. The first locomotive entered traffic in 1988, but several were later converted to 'freight only' working. Seen at Preston in January 2005, 90026 is one of the batch that had their Electric Train Heating equipment removed.*

Understandably, there were many amendments, some technical but others involving serious points of substance, including guarantees of control over fares and the protection for special groups. A Rail Regulator was appointed, and his statutory powers came into effect in April 1994 by which time a 'matrix' had been established for shadow running of the railways, still under the ownership of British Rail but with responsibility for privatisation resting with the Government.

Left: *Privatisation of a kind came to the Worth Valley Railway, when it was re-opened as a Light Railway in 1968. In the upper view Ivatt 2-6-2T 41212, painted in the railway's livery runs services on the day of re-opening. Three decades later, when the lower view was taken in 1998, the line had become a popular tourist attraction. Not only did it see the use of steam trains, like the ex-LNWR 'Coal Tank', but also regular diesel traction.*

The process of privatising the passenger train operators was not completed until April 1997, a month before the General Election, but Railtrack had been privatised in 1996 and the operating companies well before that. The principle of private companies operating on a state-owned railway track network is easily understood, after all, it is directly in line with the way the state provides the road network for the general public to use at large, but then gets its returns via direct and in-direct taxation. Some sections of the road network are maintained at a great loss to the exchequer, but done so on the grounds of social necessity.

The 'Big Four' railway companies argued that this should be the case back in 1947, even though their argument was overlooked and the whole rail system nationalised. Fifty years of state-ownership did not decrease the validity of those 1947 arguments. Had the Conservatives been content with simply privatising the railway operating companies, these may well have been an adequate way to address the future needs of the nation, but instead they chose to sell off the track and infrastructure business (which they called Railtrack) as well.

For many railway analysts, historians, enthusiasts and employees this was a sell-off too far, and what was basically a very rich property-owning company was 'given' to the private sector with very little return to the state. Ironically, despite being handed the 'family silver on a golden platter', Railtrack went into administration and saw its shares suspended only five years after privatisation.

What is more, several executives and contractors potentially faced criminal charges over safety matters, as Railtrack looked to recruit its third Chief Executive in a twelve-month period and was in as much trouble as a firm could be. All of this begs the question, "Why did this last major Conservative privatisation fail so singularly when others (such as water, telephones, gas and electricity) more or less, succeeded?" Did this mean that there were lessons about the natural limits for hiving off public sector activity, or did the mode adopted for restructuring the railway industry make this case unique?

Certain explanations can be discounted, such as the immediate costs of the traffic disruption caused by the accidents but, the main question, 'was Railtrack mismanaged', is much harder to answer! Its Board were undoubtedly diverted from the core business of providing a safe, well-managed railway infrastructure in favour of exploiting the property portfolio; in other words selling off the family silver in smaller lots at a huge profit!

Some say that this was a pre-condition of its privatisation and an understandable reaction to market expectations, as well as a means of rewarding the shareholders. Yet, few can disagree with the view that Railtrack mismanaged its responsibility of railway maintenance, making the classical errors of adopting the wrong form of contract for complex activity (fixed cost, loose objectives).

Top Right: *By the 1990s, many grand station buildings were simply vandalised shells. A classic example of the neglect is seen on the Up platform at Lytham & St. Anne's Station near the seaside resort of Blackpool in 1993.*

Bottom Right: *Conversely, some stations were completely re-vamped by Railtrack in an attempt to re-capture tourist traffic. Take for instance the superb junction station at Hellifield in North Yorkshire, which was restored to recapture some of its Victorian splendour.*

Above: Safety was of course the big issue facing Railtrack, and little confidence was placed in the organisation, despite the fact that it had a vast wealth of experience to call upon from former BR staff. The BR Technical Centre had collected much data on accidents, including this one staged with a nuclear flask at the Old Dalby Test Track, with Peak Class 46009 on 17th July 1984.

Railtrack also underestimated the engineering requirements and cost of contract management, as well as failing to exercise the system-wide safety leadership expected by the rail users (both passengers and train operating companies).

All this rightly attracted strong criticism, although the most important measures (railway safety) did actually improve under Railtrack on the whole. The failures of the management may well have passed unnoticed in most industries, and they were remediable, but it was the fragmentation of the control of the rail system that was the central failure!

As a prelude to the sell off, railway operations had been split into 'sectors', or separate businesses operating within British Rail. As a result of this fragmentation and de-centralisation of management, a number of problems became evident. Most significant of these was the rift between the control of track and the operation of trains, as this certainly did not assist safety. It reduced feedback between operating elements (e.g. signallers and drivers), and introduced problems with safety leadership that Railtrack spectacularly failed to solve. Crucially, it lent itself to serious under-estimation of the need for common arrangements. For instance they failed to introduce a proper framework for technical development and systems management and ignored an industry-wide approach to developing what had become scarce expertise. This seems a complete travesty, given that the railways had always been both institutional and organisational, in the early days modelling themselves on the management techniques of the armed forces.

Top Right: We have previously mentioned the problems of public perception that followed Beeching, as the railways became the butt of many a stand-up comedians' joke in the 1970s and '80s. Yet, there was little wonder when passengers were forced to travel long distances, such as on this two-car DMU leaving Barnstaple for Exeter in 1986, in antiquated, often dirty, and supremely uncomfortable rolling stock.

Bottom Right: However, some significant changes were seen in the DMU fleet during the late-1980s and early-1990s, especially with Class 158 DMUs. Built by BREL at Derby, with their airline seating and air-conditioning, the 158s can be seen operating in many parts of the country. They have a top speed of 90mph and are thus ideal for long journeys such as this Liverpool - York train pictured at Todmorden in 1992.

Over the hundred years between Stephenson and the Grouping of 1923, the railways had developed schools of excellence in every single technical arena. These naturally included the fields of mechanical and civil engineering, but much more besides. The railways had their own chemists, paint analysts, electrical engineers, gas producers, brick-makers, and schools of signalling, maritime navigation, road vehicle driving and hotel management to name but a few. Importantly there was also a tradition of sons following their fathers (grandfathers and so on) into railway employ, so that even raw recruits had a good grounding in their chosen profession. To many, knowing the railway rule book off by heart was more important than schooling!

Post-Beeching the driving force of invention began to disappear from BR, as employees took the view that it was 'better to do nothing than be criticised for doing something and possibly failing'. As a result many skills fell through the cracks and therefore have now to be expensively re-invented as we start a possible period of railway expansion at the start of the 21st century.

Top Left: *In 1976 British Rail decided that it would need new locomotives for the Merry-go-Round coal trains within a very short time. The contract was awarded to Brush Traction, who decided to use a modified Class 47 bodyshell and a Ruston-Paxman power unit. Yet, due to a lack of capacity at their Loughborough factory, Brush sub-contracted the work to Electroputere at Craiova, Romania. The first Rumanian loco, 56006 entered service in 1976, but after the first 30 locomotives were delivered, BR decided that it would build future locomotives to the same design itself! The first British Class 56 (56031), was the first of 105 locomotives to be built at either the BREL works in Crewe or Doncaster. Here we see 56057 on a bulk waste transfer train at Bedford in 1990.*

Bottom Left: *The Class 58s were the last locomotives to be designed and built by British Rail at Doncaster Works between 1983 and 1987. The first locomotive was 58001, seen here at Crewe in December 1983. They were designed for freight-only work and thus fitted with just air brakes and slow-speed control. The class were a breakthrough in design terms and allocated to Toton depot.* British Rail Engineering Ltd.

Nevertheless, this fragmentation did seem to provide the managerial focus and customer-driven approach that were the *raison-d'etre* for privatisation. For instance the new locomotive and rolling stock leasing companies, having made huge profits from what was massively under-valued rolling stock at the time of their sale, are now bringing in fresh capital and better engineering maintenance. Some say this is helping to sharpen the manufacturing sector, but very few trains are made in Britain these days and the importation of other nation's products is a travesty for the land that invented railways in the first place. Although Railtrack and the other debacles have landed during a Labour government's administration, the faults cannot be properly laid on the doorstep of Mr. Blair in Downing Street.

When his party came to power in 1997 no railway assets remained in the public sector but very few powers of control remained for the Government as the franchises were then running on contracts of seven years (or longer) settled by the Franchising Director.

Privatisation has seen some improvements taking place, but a series of scandals and serious accidents, along with complaints that Railtrack plc cared more about their profits than the safety of their users, ultimately led to the operation being effectively taken back into state control. Today, the network is roughly the same size as it was 30 years ago in 1975 (12,000 miles of track and 2,000 stations) whereas 50 years ago (in 1955) it had 20,000 miles of track and 6,000 stations.

It is difficult to present a view of where the next century will take the railways here in Britain, especially given the fact that during the Thatcher administration of the 1980s, Britain lost its edge in the world of railway technology. Today we must re-invent those skills or import them from overseas. Yet some new key players have taken positive steps in the railways of the future. Take GNER who have proved to be so effective in their operation of the East Coast Main Line, or Sir Richard Branson's Virgin Trains operation that turned the shambolic West Coast route around following years of under-investment. His new fleet of Pendolino trains have certainly improved the passenger comfort standards on the longer WCML journey, which owes so much to Stephenson's involvement in the 1830s and '40s.

Top Right: *Inter-City 125 High Speed Trains, were introduced on 4th October 1976. The first London-Bristol service arrived three minutes early, and for four decades they have continued front line duties such as these seen leaving Penzance, Britain's most south-westerly station, in 1996.*

Bottom Right: *Light rail, such as the Manchester scheme offers much hope for advances in local rapid transport systems.*

Above: *Some schemes have taken a positive step towards a new initiative in railway operation, and between 1990 and 1996, I was involved in advising the government on how they could help local communities 're-invent the wheel' by taking over the control of their railway and running it themselves. One scheme I was intimately involved with was the Weardale Railway, which was eventually sold off by Railtrack to a private company limited by guarantee. Here we see the inspection saloon, behind 31547 as it is being used to show the line to its prospective buyers fittingly at the terminal point of the Stockton & Darlington Railway in Shildon on 18th May 1993. Somehow or another, the Weardale scheme lost its impetus and did not re-open until the summer of 2004 - a few months later it was sadly placed in administration.*

Is there then a future for rail? The answer has to be yes, especially if we are to act on the environmentally-friendly form of mass transit they so clearly can provide. Forty years of neglect by successive governments from 1963 to 2003 cannot and will not be put right in just the few years following privatisation. We are essentially still in the early days of privatisation, but many take the view that private operation can only be achieved by putting profits ahead of passengers. Are they right to hold such a view, or will privatisation pay its due dividends for society as well as shareholders?

Certainly the unprofitable rural rail routes will be victims if this philosophy continues, and as the end of 200 Years of Rail was reached, The Observer newspaper commented on the matter by using the Penistone line as a classic example.

"Rail experts say the axing of Britain's worst-performing services is long overdue. Subsidies for all rail services have ballooned to more than £4bn a year. Could it even be time, some whisper, to launch a Beeching II cutback? ....After decades facing the threat of cuts, the futures of the Penistone line and the rest of Britain's much-loved but little-used rural railways may soon be decided. Such an exercise would be guaranteed to trigger another bitter battle between the countryside and officialdom, for despite the closed waiting rooms, freezing carriages and lack of staff, most rural communities see their rail services as a precious lifeline, an environmentally friendly alternative to cars and a relaxing way to enjoy the most beautiful stretches of British countryside. They will bitterly oppose closures.

Nevertheless, the outlook is grim. The Transport Department's strategy promises to halve the subsidy spent on relaying each passenger along miles of quiet track - saving about £300m. A key change will be asking local groups to help market services, and even help with basic maintenance - an initiative pioneered by the Penistone line.

But at the same time, the Office of the Rail Regulator has revealed it is carrying out a massive exercise in pinpointing the cost of running many of these lines to 'assess the impact on infrastructure costs of changes in service patterns'. Last year, the ten most subsidised services used nearly two-thirds of the total £2bn subsidy bill to operators. This is on top of the billions in government grants awarded to Network Rail. While rail supporters say cutting rural services would make little impact on the company's costs, others point to the expense of a bigger bureaucracy and more complicated procurement.

Critics also say that saving even a few hundred million pounds a year is important, when a few years ago a £50m freight grant scheme to ease congested roads, was cut because of funding problems. 'Multiply that over ten years and you could build an awful lot of hospitals, extra railways, do a lot of other things,' added one industry executive. There is also almost no record of passenger numbers on rural railways, let alone of the wider social and economic benefits. And what evidence there is is not promising." Yet the revival of rail routes like the Settle & Carlisle line can only be to the good of the rural areas through which these trains travel, and to the environment as a whole.

Better passenger services with more friendly, customer-oriented staff will surely pay their own dividends. New trains, such as the Pendolino sets or the newer, more comfortable units appearing on local services auger well for the future, but the investment has to continue these improvements. Furthermore, the re-opening of closed lines and stations must be undertaken as a priority, in order for railways to socially serve the communities in which they operate. Perhaps the most fitting example of this 'community' approach, is that seen running through Wensleydale, North Yorkshire, which is a really good blueprint for others to follow.

Two centuries ago, we tamed the Iron Monster and for a long while we kept it under control, but it was then left on a very loose leash, and finally set upon by ignorant people fearful of its power. We now need to repair what has been damaged before and then strive to create a system that works for the common good, as well as provide a bit of fun for those boys (and girls) who never really want to grow up !

Below: *One of the new Virgin Pendolino tilting train sets, is seen at Preston in December 2004.*

In Conclusion

Any book such as this owes its genesis to a large number of people, historians and photographers, who have helped (sometimes unwittingly) in its compilation. To name all those who have helped me in my journey through 200 years of railway history would be a physical impossibility. Yet, one person who stands out more than all the others is the late-David Jenkinson, who was a mentor to me in more ways than one; both in his days at the National Railway Museum in York and latterly as a book publisher and fellow railway company Director. It is now some ten years since we talked of my doing a series of books on railway history, but I hope that the final result is something he would have been pleased with, so it is with deep gratitude that I dedicate this book to his memory.

Above: *This picture, which sums up the on-going interest in railway history, was taken from the bottom of my garden on 1st May 2005, as BR Standard Class 8P 4-6-0 71000, waits to depart from Appleby. This unique locomotive was built after the Harrow & Wealdstone disaster of 1952 destroyed ex-LMS engine* Princess Anne. *Accordingly, Robert Riddles, the last great steam locomotive designer, set out to build a new prototype for the future. In 1954 71000,* Duke Of Gloucester, *came out of Derby Works as the first of a new generation of express steam engines, which would serve British Railways until the network was completely electrified. Yet by 1962, and with steam being replaced by diesel traction, 71000 was declared surplus and listed for preservation, but in 1965 it was condemned to the scrap instead. A strange twist of fate saw it languishing at Barry, South Wales until 1973, when it was rescued and finally restored by 1986 despite many obstacles.*